SOCIAL SKILLS MADE EASY

HOW TO TALK TO ANYONE

PROVEN STRATEGIES FOR MASTERING SMALL TALK, CONFIDENT SPEAKING, APPROACHABLE COMMUNICATION, AND NETWORKING SUCCESS

JACK WOLF

BOOK ONE:
LIFE SCULPTOR BLUEPRINT SERIES

https://posg.life

POSG, Inc.
https://posg.life

Contents

Desperate for Breakthough
Introduction

Of all the dumb luck and irony in the world, I felt like I got randomly and genetically cheated at conception.

I am an intelligent, insightful, fascinating, witty, and fun person to engage with, yet I was also naturally born a timid introvert. Having conversations was not only outside the realm of possibility within my closed universe; I would have been ecstatic if I could simply make eye contact with another person for more than one second before lowering my head and turning red. Then came the other symptoms: I would lose all concentration or ability to hold a meaningful thought, I would start sweating profusely, an irrational and unexplainable fear would wash over me, and I would suddenly devalue everything I ever experienced and ever loved. In those moments, the only thing I could focus on would be leaving the area and finding relief from the storm in my physiology.

Does this sound familiar? Do you struggle to a greater or lesser degree to engage in playful, open, or profoundly meaningful discussions with others? What is it about public speaking that so many of us fear?

I found the solution. I got free of that dreaded physiological storm. I can now hold eye contact and converse with anyone with joy and freedom. I learned through years of effort and practice the best and worst ways to address social anxiety and win the battle over the physical and emotional effects of fear.

I am now an entrepreneur, author, and public speaker with years of experience as a large enterprise technology salesperson. Imagine that.

How does a shy person lead discussions in the executive boardroom with the influential decision-makers of large enterprise companies?

My life has found a fresh purpose. I have to lead others to the same waters I drank from. I must offer the lessons learned in my biggest struggle to other people sharing similar stories.

Of course, I can't make you drink, but I can help you find your way. You have to drink for yourself. You must be willing to let go of your control and accept some concepts on blind faith alone until they become reality.

But could it work?

Dave, a 32-year-old from central Illinois, may have presented as shy and socially anxious on the outside, but what he wanted to be was confident and outgoing. He grew up in an environment made of anxiety, criticism, and negativity and found himself trapped in the shadow of his insecurity. Despite these challenges, Dave sought social skills tools to begin his transformation. Using these tools, along with patience and persistence, he would discover the strengths he already had that he could leverage to help overcome his social anxiety.

Armed with practical and actionable strategies, like those you will discover in this book, Dave began to break through barriers of social anxiety that had been holding him back for years. He confronted his fears and negative thought patterns and focused on improving his social skills to make interacting with others easier. He started experiencing improvements, both big and small.

One day, he decided to join his coworkers regularly for lunch, a habit that helped him develop better professional relationships. This improvement led to more significant breakthroughs, and he began forming more meaningful relationships and deeper personal connections. He even started dating and pursuing a more long-term romantic relationship!

Through the setbacks and successes, Dave kept his goal in sight and was able to break free from his social anxiety. It was work, but it became fun work. He relaxed and allowed himself to live a life of connection and fulfillment. His story is a shining example that with courage and willingness to take risks, the possibilities for transformation are limitless.

Are you also experiencing anxiety surrounding communication and social situations? These anxieties turn into a fear of rejection, a fear of public speaking, and feelings of inadequacy when in social situations. As a result, you might only enter social situations partially and with much reservation. Even if you don't struggle with anxiety, you may be struggling with your communication and social skills, like initiating conversations with new people. If you want to avoid being held back from social opportunities because you struggle with communication and social skills, then the information in this book can help you begin your transformation, just like Dave.

This book's tips, strategies, and advice can help you overcome. When you lack confidence in your communication skills, you may stumble over words, worry about saying the wrong thing, or fall silent in social situations. This book will help you gain the confidence you need to thrive socially. From this book, you will discover:

How To Lay The Social Groundwork—The first three chapters will explore how to embrace your unique and authentic self! The first step to overcoming social anxiety and improving social skills is self-discovery and learning to love yourself. You'll learn to overcome social anxiety and boost your self-esteem and confidence in social situations.

How to Develop Practical Social and Communication Skills - If you need practical advice for improving your social and communication skills, you'll want to pay special attention to Part Two. Conversation is an art, and you'll learn how to master it, including how to start and maintain a high-quality conversation. But talking to others is just half of a conversation; you'll also learn the valuable skills of active listening.

Remember that listening to someone else's words, reading their body language, and using non-verbal strategies are essential to clarifying communication and enhancing a conversation.

How to Use Revolutionary Communication Tactics to Transform Your Communication—In the final section, you learn how to go beyond maintaining a conversation and use revolutionary communication tactics to take your communication skills to the next level. You'll learn how to use empathy and emotional intelligence to build and strengthen relationships, set effective boundaries respectfully, cultivate trust in relationships, and effectively network and forge professional relationships.

Like Dave and me, you can use this book to leave your social anxiety behind. It will help you discover how to communicate and forge relationships with confidence and ease. It will help you to help others find the same freedom and success that you will enjoy.

By the end of it, you'll be starting and upholding interesting conversations with absolutely anyone!

***

Note:

I have included break-outs for action throughout this book. I encourage you to make massive efforts and take leaps of faith toward your personal progress. While you do not have to do these action steps, you will find that they are designed to either unlock hope or shift subconscious limiting beliefs to the forefront so you can confront them. Fear gains power whenever we allow it to convince us not to act. So, acting despite fear is a powerful tool for serving eviction papers to any that may be holding you back at present. From this day forward, please agree to press ahead and be free.

FREE GIFT

I have a special gift for you. You've finished reading the introduction, so you know a little bit about me. This book focuses on helping people break free of fear, shyness, and social anxiety to learn to talk to anyone. It is possible to learn to love the process.

Visit the link below and enter your email address, and I'll instantly send you a link to my **Super-Secret Resources Page**. It's effortless and will amaze you.

You'll receive a few more emails with all the additional content I promised throughout the book. This includes some unique advanced training, custom content to further your journey in Talking To Anyone, Opportunities for quitting your job and becoming an entrepreneur, and even more insider strategies for transformational success.

Break out with extreme momentum. Supercharge your results today to accelerate your growth. You can turn down the volume of social anxiety and experience the thrill of increasing control over your life and talking to anyone.

https://posg.life/GetSecretAccess

Part I: Laying Down the Social Groundwork
Chapters 1 – 3

"The truly scary thing about undiscovered lies is that they have a greater capacity to diminish us than exposed ones. They erode our strength, our self-esteem, our very foundation." -**Cheryl Hughes**

Chapter 1
Embracing Your Unique and Authentic Self

There once was a depressing voice that spoke darkly in my soul. It often told me, "You are the only one who knows how absolutely wretched and unlovable you really are." The voice was insatiable and inescapable. So, I walked through life with a mask to keep people at a distance. I couldn't change my reality, but I could do my utmost to keep others from discovering it.

Do you ever feel like you're walking through life wearing a mask? Do you feel the need to hide your true self because you're afraid of ridicule or unacceptance? If you do, I first want this book to tell you you're not alone. Everyone is living with varying degrees of comfort about letting their authentic personality shine for all to see. Some always do. Some never do.

And that's the second thing I want this book to tell you: You don't have to be that person wearing the mask. You can be you, no matter what other people think. What matters most is that YOU accept and embrace yourself; others can take it or leave it. And the ones who leave it? It's no big loss.

This may sound simplistic, and perhaps you've already saddled yourself with the self-limiting belief that no one will accept the real you. This chapter is designed to show you that you're wrong (in the best possible way!) The only opinion that matters is your own, and we'll discuss how you can open yourself up to the world by taking charge of your confidence and how you can use that authenticity to tackle any social situation with grace and poise. When you are living your best, authentic life, it makes it that much easier to manage social activities—you'll find that conversation flows better, you'll have more confidence to speak your mind and stand your ground, and you'll begin to relate to people on your terms, rather then feeling as if you need to let them set the tone.

Consider the story of Julia, a woman in her early 30s struggling with body image issues, an eating disorder, and a husband who never gave her any reason to believe that she had worth. And so, she didn't. When the husband eventually called it quits on her, and she ended up hospitalized for not eating correctly, something clicked. Not only did Julia realize that she needed to take serious strides to improve her mental and physical health, but she also realized that the root of her issues was low self-esteem caused by worrying too much about what other people saw when they looked at her.

That day, Julia promised herself that she would no longer let the power of other people's opinions impact how she lived her life. She may have been feeling at her lowest, but she would use this experience as a stepping stone to a new, improved, AUTHENTIC life. Fast-forward to today. Julia is thriving in a new career, building positive relationships, and seeing her therapist regularly to support her recovery from her eating disorder. How did she get from such a low Point A to the heights of Point B? Persistence, self-belief, and embracing her own uniqueness. Let's talk about how you can do the same.

The Importance of Self-Acceptance

First things first, let's give ourselves a working definition of self-acceptance. Let's go with this one:

> True self-acceptance is embracing yourself without
> qualifications, conditions, or exceptions (The Path to
> Unconditional Self-Acceptance, n.d.).

So, what does that really mean? To begin with, it means that we must embrace ourselves, flaws and all. It doesn't mean we can't change those flaws and work on becoming our best selves. Self-acceptance can be an incredible starting point for personal growth because self-acceptance begins with honesty. To be authentic with others, you must first be authentic to yourself.

People who succeed at being self-accepting exhibit confidence without conceit, admit weaknesses and faults without being overly critical, and have the self-respect and clarity to see themselves as whole, without the need for the approval of others. It can seem like a tall order, especially if you're coming from a place where you feel small. Consider some scenarios where self-acceptance might come into play, affecting everyday life, such as in the workplace.

Scenario 1: Your supervisor asks you to take on a new project, but it requires a diverse skill set to complete. If you are someone who doesn't accept yourself, you might be afraid to take the project, focusing only on the sections you feel are out of your depth and confirming to yourself why you should turn down the project. All points converge on the reality that you don't accept yourself enough to believe you can do it. If you are someone who does accept yourself, you will have the confidence to say that you can take it on, knowing that there are some facets of the work with which you may need some assistance or training to accomplish appropriately. Parsing that self-acceptance into authenticity means you can truthfully express this reality to your supervisor.

Scenario 2: You must deliver a presentation on a new product to a significant client, but public speaking isn't your forte. If you can accept and embrace that it's not a strength for you, you can plan to practice and deliver a presentation in a way that feels comfortable and doable for you. If you're not self-accepting, you might fight off or resist preparing adequately because you'll feel like the whole presentation is doomed from the start. This can lead to a self-fulfilling prophecy of failure because you're so wrapped up in worrying what others will think of you—meaning you won't put in the practice that will give you the confidence to do your best and not care what they think.

After reading those two scenarios, which person would you rather be? The one who embraces their 'weaknesses' and gives themselves the tools to be confident, or the one who shrinks away for fear of failure? These are natural consequences of not being self-accepting, which can lead to a struggle to succeed in your career and personal life. When you can't embrace your true self—the good and the bad—you can't reach your full potential. You become bogged down by self-doubt and low self-esteem and begin to accumulate what we all so lovingly refer to as 'emotional baggage.' Kidding aside, when you can't or don't practice self-acceptance, you're doing a grave disservice to your mental health. You could find yourself dealing with anxiety, depression, eating disorders, unhealthy substance dependencies, and other concerns. And that's no way to live your best life.

When you *can* practice self-acceptance, you can truly begin to live a more positive, confident lifestyle. You'll become more resilient when faced with obstacles or criticism. You'll become better at forgiving yourself for errors and more self-congratulatory when you achieve a goal or accomplishment. These things are critical to healing from past wounds and traumas, forging new paths for yourself, and living authentically every day.

Practicing Self-Acceptance

Let's talk about some ways that you can practice becoming more self-accepting. The more whole you become, the better the experiences and encounters you will have as you authentically present yourself and practice the methods of "How to Talk to Anyone":

Embrace your values: Your values are what make you uniquely you. These principles you live on include your morals, ethics, personality traits, and even religious beliefs. Your values guide your decision-making and color the way you see the world. When you are not self-accepting, especially of your values, it can seem tempting to 'betray' those values and make decisions based on what others might think, even if it doesn't feel right to you. An example of this might be a teenager who accepts a cigarette or alcohol from a friend, even though they are personally uncomfortable with breaking the rules about underage usage. The teenager allows himself to be more concerned about the opinions of others than standing up for his values.

Forgive yourself for past mistakes: It's so easy to beat ourselves up. Isn't it? The internet is chock-full of memes and quips depicting people thinking about the past while trying to sleep or playfully calling out the human habit of hypothetically finishing arguments while alone in the shower. The truth is that it's incredibly challenging to forgive ourselves for the things we could have, would have, and should have done differently. We allow ourselves to be haunted by the ghosts of unhappy conversations, unhealthy relationships, and destructive behaviors. As Elsa would say, "Let it go." To be genuinely self-accepting, you need to be able to recognize two things: the past is done and can't be undone, and not too many things in this world are genuinely unforgivable. Forgive yourself. Move forward. It'll be okay.

Avoid self-blame: Not everything is your fault. Seriously. Blaming ourselves for the world's woes doesn't change the world's woes. Have you ever caught yourself apologizing for things entirely outside of your control? That's something that self-acceptance can help with. You can only control yourself. You cannot control the weather. You cannot control the tides. You cannot control other people. What they do is 100 percent their decision, and if something goes awry, it's 100 percent not your fault. It's almost easier to take the blame on your shoulders so that people will like you, but if it's not something directly caused by something you did or said (or didn't do or didn't say), then it's not your fault.

Prevent comparisons: Everyone writes their own story, and no one will share the same narrative. Don't compare yourself or your journey to that of others. It's a trap many people fall into—and we start young! Who got better grades on a test, got the new trendy outfit, made the football team, and got into what college? And then we get to adulthood, and it's cars and jobs and houses and spouses. It's a lot! Step back, take a deep breath, and appreciate and accept what you have as part of your unique story. If you're unhappy about something, don't frame it as "I want this because so-and-so already has it." Instead, ask yourself what the true benefit of having that thing would be, and if it's truly something that will make your life better or more whole, then you can plan to achieve it.

Stop caring: Literally, stop caring. Your inner dialogue will try to make you care about what others will think about you. It will try to convince you that you are misunderstood or unaccepted. You have to realize that you are the Alpha in charge of your own life. No one else can have that control. Allow others' influence over the real estate of your thoughts, emotions, and decisions to be downgraded from "Highly Impactful" to "Ankle-Biter" status. You must no longer claim the responsibility of being a people pleaser.

Be more mindful: There are entire books written on the topic of mindfulness. And its practice benefits many areas of life beyond the subject of self-acceptance. However, mindfulness is about awareness, and self-awareness can lead to greater self-acceptance. Be present in your activities. Be aware of what is happening now, not what's already happened and what could happen in the future. Being mindful helps you be more aware of your behaviors and the behaviors of those around you, which allows you to come to realize something: you may be worried about what others think of you, but you'll notice that they're pretty wrapped up in themselves. You'll also begin to notice patterns in the behaviors of those people, which can lead you to our next tip.

Seek and question your patterns: When you become aware enough to notice the behavioral patterns of others, you should also become aware of your behavioral patterns, both separate and in conjunction with your relationships. How do you act when you're alone? How do you react to the behavior of others? How do you behave over the long term when faced with specific scenarios? You may come to realize that you become overly apologetic for no reason. Perhaps you observe a pattern of self-destructive behavior when you come up against obstacles because it's easier to set yourself up for failure than to just 'let it happen.' Question yourself. Ask, "Why do I behave this way?" If you find that a specific behavior is problematic or stands in the way of self-acceptance and confidence, ask yourself what steps you need to take to make positive changes.

Make a habit of self-acceptance: Reaching the point of self-acceptance isn't quite enough to call yourself self-accepting. You must make a habit of it. You'll slowly but surely become self-accepting by consistently correcting your detrimental behaviors, practicing mindfulness and positive self-talk, and accepting who you are. When self-acceptance becomes a habit, you can truly embrace being an authentic, unique person.

If you build a consistent, habitual cycle of utilizing these tips, self-acceptance can and will become easier for you until, one day, it may feel like you never struggled with it all.

If you need more assistance with confronting and adjusting your habits, please read my book **Transformational Success Habits: A 30-Day Plan to Take Charge of Your Struggles in Personal Growth, Leadership Skills, and Finances**. This book is a power-packed journey into the science of habits, describing how you can hack the biological function of habits to sculpt your life into the person you desire to be. Find more details at https://posg.life/habits

Celebrating Your Uniqueness and Authenticity

Once you can accept yourself in all your authentic glory, that's when the fun begins. If you no longer care about anyone's opinion but your own, you can truly start to let your personality shine. (Note: Some societal norms still apply, and tastefulness is a treasure rather than a bothersome limitation. Don't go to your office job in a bikini or sing raunchy drinking songs at a funeral. Unless, of course, the deceased was the lead singer of a raunchy drinking song band.)

So, what is authenticity? Here's one definition from the psychology perspective:

Individuals considered authentic are those who strive to align their actions with their core values and beliefs with the hope of discovering and then acting in sync with their true selves (Authenticity | Psychology Today United Kingdom, n.d.).

You may wish to read that again.

Some researchers have suggested that authenticity can be determined by four criteria: self-awareness, unbiased processing of one's strengths and weaknesses, behavior aligned with one's core values, and orientation within interpersonal relationships. That sounds like what we just discussed about self-acceptance. Doesn't it?

When you can embrace and celebrate your authenticity, you'll feel like a weight has been lifted off your shoulders. Remember that mask in the first sentence of this chapter? You won't have to wear it anymore. You'll have the confidence to show off your true face without hiding behind a mask that you think others will find more pleasing. Continuing to practice self-acceptance helps you remove and keep the mask off.

You'll also find that you're better at regulating your emotions and reactions to people and situations around you. When you're not spending emotional energy worrying about how things might happen or how people will react to you, you can spend that emotional energy regulating your feelings and actions. It will feel like such a relief when you only have one person's emotions to worry about regulating, meaning yours.

Another amazing aspect of authenticity is the ability to embrace and display your uniqueness. Instead of hiding or masking your differences, you can proudly say, "This is who I am, and I love me for it!" Celebrating what makes you unique can boost your creativity and self-expression and help you contribute to a more diverse society. It also enables you to continue to build your self-confidence and practice self-acceptance.

Let's explore some ways you can become more comfortable with your uniqueness and tell the world, "This is me!"

Get to know yourself: Spend time with yourself! What do you like about yourself? What bothers you? What are your values? Journaling is an excellent tool for getting to know yourself better, but you can also try mindfulness and meditation exercises. Even personality type tests can help you better handle what makes you tick. The point is that some people don't actually own their values and preferences. Instead, they allow others to shape them. Be structurally sound in who you are and who you aren't.

Find your passions: When thinking about your passions, a good question to ask yourself is this: If you had to give a 30-minute speech on any topic right now, with no time to prepare, what would you talk about? Also, consider what activities or entertainment options you look forward to most in your spare time. Do you have causes you like to champion? These are all things to think about.

Embrace your quirks: Quirky is good! Without quirks, we'd all be boring people in a dull world. If you have a quirk that's not hurting anyone, including yourself, then go for it. Do you like to eat chocolate ice cream with Doritos®? Go for it. Have to have the TV volume on an even number? Cool. Never wear matching socks? You rebel you. Quirks make life more enjoyable; yours deserve their time in the sun. Let your quirks season your discussions with others. Generally, conversations lack honesty if we only allow others to see a perfect presentation of ourselves.

Take risks:

1. *Apply* for the dream job.

2. Go skydiving.

3. Learn to surf.

4. Take yourself to dinner, and don't worry if other people wonder where your date is.

You and your uniqueness can try so many new adventures.

Wear clothes that make you feel confident: You're the only person inside your clothing at any given time, so who cares what other people think of it? If you love it, wear it. (See the above note about societal norms.) If you find the perfect dress and can't think of another person who would wear it, that's great! That means that the dress is unique to you. Buy it. Wear it. Rock it. Love it.

Be kind: This is the Golden Rule. Treat others like you'd like to be treated, even if it isn't always reciprocated. You never know what someone else is going through, and your kind words and actions may be the ticket to turning their day around.

Focus on your personal growth and progress: This goes back to self-acceptance and not comparing yourself to others. Stay focused on you, your goals, and your progress. No one else's path is the same as yours, meaning you only have to concentrate on your own.

Recognize and value your unique talents and abilities: Everyone is exceptional regarding at least one thing. Whether that's artistic or intellectual talent, an aptitude for sports, baking cheesecakes, or knowing what to gift a friend for their birthday, recognize and value your powers. They are part of what makes you uniquely you.

Celebrate your unique perspective and those of others: If you want to be heard, listen. Part of being an exceptional person with a unique perspective and experience is listening to that of others. We can learn so much about the world from each other when we stop, listen, and truly hear what we all have to offer. Celebrate your perspective and give space and consideration to those of other people.

Recognize personal strengths and weaknesses: Acknowledging your strengths isn't bragging, and recognizing your weaknesses isn't admitting defeat. These things don't need to be extreme to be valid or invalid, but knowing where you excel and where you may have some skill gaps is valuable knowledge for planning and achieving personal growth.

Reflect on life experiences and values: Look for the connection between your experiences, decisions, and value set. Connecting the dots will give you greater insight into your behavioral patterns so you can showcase your uniqueness without going against the core of your beliefs and values.

Embrace vulnerability and work on overcoming your fear of judgment: Seriously. Take yourself out to dinner. It'll be delicious, and you'll have more room on the table to spread your dinner and bread plates. The point here is to learn to accept the uncomfortable within. Let the inner turmoil of uncomfortable situations wash over you until they lose their power.

Time for Some Action!
Embrace Your Quirks: Choose one personal quirk and celebrate it in a conversation or on social media.

Authentic Self vs. Adaptive Self

Your adaptive self will occasionally rear its head, even if you live your most authentic life. Your adaptive self is the side of you that bends or concedes to things that may go against the truth your authentic self wants to live. This can be healthy or unhealthy, depending on the situation. If you feel like being authentic could harm your physical safety or well-being, you can put the mask back on and be adaptive for as long as it takes to get you out of harm's way.

There are other times when being adaptive is beneficial, such as NOT wearing a bikini to your office job. While your authentic self may want to live in beachwear, following the company dress code will help you stay employed. Being deliberate about when you should push for authenticity and when you should step back and be adaptive is a massive part of being genuinely self-accepting. You don't want to risk getting stuck back in your non-self-accepting ways and having to do the work all over again. Developing your authenticity and making room for your uniqueness take time; avoid losing it by being too adaptive when it isn't called for.

To maintain your authenticity, be discerning. Make a habit of telling the truth, but please remember to be kind. Telling the truth doesn't have to come at the expense of hurting others. Be thoughtful and conscientious in your decision-making to stay true to yourself and your values, and develop yourself authentically. There is always room for self-improvement.

Using Individuality to Aid You in Social Situations

No one lives on an island, no matter how authentic or unique they are. What I mean by that is that we are all part of a larger group—we have family, friends, neighbors, colleagues, and a greater society to which we belong. That means we must reckon with our authentic selves within the larger whole.

The culture we grow up with and immerse ourselves in as adults doesn't always match, nor does it have to. If you were raised in a strictly religious household but chose a different religion or no religion as an adult, that's a change in culture and context. If you grew up in a predominantly ethnically homogenous country and then moved to a melting pot like the United States for college or work, culture shock may set in quickly. But here's the cool thing about self-acceptance, authenticity, and uniqueness—these self-concepts can help shape who we are, who we become, and how we can find our place in whatever society we choose or find ourselves in.

Self-identity and group identity are not mutually exclusive, but they can be mutually beneficial. You can be true to yourself and adore who you are while also enjoying being part of a larger group. Lots of different people make up a sports team, and while together, those people might identify themselves as football players. When the team isn't on the field, they are individuals who enjoy cooking, reading, playing video games, hiking, and all sorts of things that make them unique.

Authenticity while still enjoying being part of a group is vital to survival as a social species. We don't have to conform to everything, but it's nice to conform to some things. It gives a sense of belonging, which all humans need and deserve. And you can do it without losing your sense of self. If there is any time that being part of a greater whole begins to impact your mental health negatively or leaves you feeling less than authentic, then it's okay to step back in self-preservation. (And yes, that applies to families, too.)

Remember to avoid comparing yourself and others when you are in a group. Doing so could impact your self-esteem—remember that being true to yourself is more vital and better for your confidence than comparing yourself to someone else. That someone else is not you, and you are not them. Instead, foster goodwill and support your friends and colleagues. Be happy for their engagements, weddings, and promotions.

Your time will come as long as you stick to your habit of self-acceptance and your path to positive growth.

Moving Forward with Self-Acceptance and Confidence

We're coming to the end of our discussion on self-acceptance and getting ready to move into our next chapter, which will address overcoming social anxiety. In that chapter, we'll build upon the concepts of self-acceptance and authenticity to help you tackle any social situation or talk to anyone. Remember to embrace your uniqueness, and let's learn how to use it to pull off even the most anxiety-inducing scenarios with grace and self-assurance.

***

Ending With a Bang!

Take massive action to gain the most impact on personal progress. Do the following as quickly as possible.

1. **Journal for Self-Discovery**: Start a journal today to explore your thoughts and feelings toward self-acceptance. If interested, you can download a free **How To Talk To Anyone** guided journal at https://posg.life/FreeDCBE. If you prefer to purchase a paperback copy, it is available on Amazon at https://posg.life/buyJournal.

2. **Challenge Your Fear:** Identify a fear that holds you back and take a small step to confront it. This will encourage you to declare war on anxiety, reminding you that it does not have a hold on you.

3. **Seek Feedback**: Ask a trusted friend or family member for honest feedback on how you present yourself authentically. Ponder their feedback and record ways you might adjust to become more authentic.

4. **Stop Caring About Others' Opinions**: Do one thing this week purely because it makes you happy, regardless of what others might think. What will it be? When will you do it?

Chapter 2
Shaking Off Those Social Anxiety Jitters

D o social situations make you nervous? Does being in a crowd or hanging out with a group give you the jitters? If so, you are not alone. Feeling nervous in new situations or where you find yourself at the center of attention is normal. People experience social anxiety jitters at different levels—from small little butterflies to big feelings that interfere with their daily lives. Public speaking, job interviews, or even going on a date will raise most people's heart rates and make them feel awkward!

Even though some anxiety is normal, it should be addressed because it prevents you from conversing with others. Suppose these feelings prevent you from enjoying your interests or forming meaningful relationships. In that case, you may want to consider what tools you can add to your mental toolbox to help you with your social anxiety so you can feel comfortable talking to anyone. In this chapter, we'll help you understand social anxiety, overcome your fears of socializing, and give you tips for easily navigating social situations.

Take Tobias Atkins, for example; he thought he was just born to be shy, and he could do nothing about it. He didn't know that Social Anxiety was a thing. He was shy and didn't have a lot of support from friends and family when learning to talk about his emotions. His social anxiety made him feel uncomfortable and awkward, and he had a hard time relaxing when he was around other people. His struggles led him to feel depressed because he wanted to be able to be himself and enjoy being with other people.

However, Tobias' life changed when he sought professional help for his social anxiety. Through a psychologist's help, he found hope, faced some hurts in his past, and began to believe that he could overcome social anxiety. He learned the tools to help him confront, frame, and process his feelings and he began to build his self-esteem. Today, Tobias is doing so well that he is assisting others to learn to develop coping skills to make living with social anxiety easier.

Understanding Social Anxiety

Social Anxiety Disorder (SAD) is a mental health condition that is characterized by an intense fear of social situations or interactions. It is also usually more long-term than occasional nervousness; it can be disruptive and prevent those suffering from it from enjoying their daily lives. The symptoms of social anxiety can vary, but some of the signs and symptoms of social anxiety include:

- In social situations, experiencing blushing, nausea, sweating, shaking, or an increased heart rate.

- Blanking out mentally or feeling your body freeze or stiff in social situations.

- Feeling embarrassed, awkward, self-conscious

- Constantly worrying about being judged, rejected, or humiliated by others in public.

- Avoid eye contact, interacting with strangers, dating, eating in front of others, or activities at school or work where you might have to be around people you don't know.

The signs and symptoms of SAD can increase or decrease over time. If you are in a new situation or experiencing other stresses in your life, your symptoms may worsen. Please note that this book is not meant to diagnose the condition; it is intended to merely discuss it for educational purposes. If you think you may be suffering from SAD, you should seek help and a diagnosis from a mental health professional.

Like with many mental health conditions, some psychologists believe that there are genetic factors that can cause someone to develop SAD. However, if your parent has been diagnosed with the condition, that doesn't necessarily mean you will also, and experts haven't been able to pinpoint a specific gene related to SAD. Some parts of the brain specifically deal with fear, such as the amygdala. If there are problems with the way these parts of the brain function, it can lead to an increase in anxiety conditions. Finally, your environment and experiences will also play a role. Certain types of traumas, bullying, or other negative social interactions can trigger SAD. It has also been said that helicopter parenting or overly strict parents can cause their children to develop social anxiety

SAD is more than just feeling shy. Feeling shy sometimes is standard for most people – if you never feel any shyness or anxiety, that in and of itself could be a different problem entirely! The difference between social anxiety and shyness is that SAD can lead to fears that disrupt your everyday life and cause you to avoid creating relationships with others. Other complications of developing social anxiety also include anxiety around interviewing for jobs, which can lead to unemployment, lack of professional growth, fear about bringing new people into your life, which can lead to isolation, addiction issues, and even depression or suicidal thoughts.

If you think you might be suffering from SAD, please seek out a professional to find relief. However, please do not settle for defeat and limit your personal growth and freedom. No one is incapable of improving their unique challenge.

Overcoming Fears About Socializing

As a young adult, my church experienced an unexpected turn of events and suddenly needed someone to lead the singing during worship. The position required that the candidate leader play an instrument and sing while guiding roughly 200 people to sing along. No one else in the church offered to volunteer. So, I quickly learned to play an electronic keyboard and sing to fill the vacancy.

I was terrified! In fact, I would physically become ill in the restroom before and after each performance. I would sweat and lose focus. I wish I had understood then what I now know about social anxiety because the manifestation of physical symptoms is tangible and disruptive. There is hope for those who understand the tools available.

Whether you have been diagnosed with SAD or simply are experiencing specific symptoms of social anxiety, there are several techniques you can use right now to help you overcome. The rest of this chapter is both for those who have a diagnosed social anxiety challenge AND for those who experience any level of nervousness around conversations outside of their comfort zone. Here are some tips and tricks to try to implement to help you cope:

Challenge your negative thoughts: If you have social anxiety, you'll know that it is easy to be weighed down by negative thoughts. Sometimes, you must challenge those thoughts head-on. Next time you have a negative thought, ask yourself if it is true and why you had the thought in the first place. Think about the base cause – is the thought based on reality or an assumption? Sometimes, you can stop a negative thought in its tracks just by challenging its existence.

Try not to focus on yourself: Someone once told me that no one thinks about me as much as I think about myself. In other words, if I walk into a room and everyone looks at me in judgment, they probably feel the same thing I am about themselves! Flip your focus, be curious, and ask about others and their lives. If you try to put yourself in others' shoes, you'll think less about how you are feeling and maybe even put some of your anxiety aside for a little while.

Stop caring: This may come as a shock to you. The idea that I am asking you not to care about the outcome or details of an engagement may sound incredibly detached or closed. However, there is an appropriate time to stone-wall anxious feelings or negative self-talk by saying in whatever language suits your personality best, "I don't care." Such an admission releases you from damaging perfectionist cycles and symptoms of anxiety. It can empower you to disallow harmful self-talk from influencing your actions or inactions. "I don't care" can give you the freedom and space to be yourself, take action, enjoy the experience, and present yourself to others.

Time for Some Action!
Adopt an 'I Don't Care' Attitude: Practice dismissing negative self-talk with an "I don't care" to reduce anxiety about outcomes. How does this approach make you feel?

Adopt healthy lifestyle habits: Taking good care of your body can be challenging when you feel bad mentally. But think about it this way - if your body feels good, it can boost your mind! Participating in healthy habits like regular exercise, getting good sleep, keeping hydrated, and eating lots of healthy, nutrient-rich foods are all great ways to take care of your body and make you feel more confident.

Take a breath: Don't underestimate the power of breathing. We are constantly breathing, but we rarely breathe deeply or with intention. Often, anxious thoughts are based on our "what ifs" and not on our reality. Taking a deep, mindful breath from your belly can center us and bring us back to the world calmer and more precise.

Act confidently: Sometimes, we must fake it until we make it! Consider how someone confident behaves and see if you can mimic those behaviors. Even if you don't feel it on the inside at first, the more you act confidently during social interactions, the more experiences you will rack up that can help build your confidence. One day, you might realize you're not mimicking anymore.

Be kind to yourself: We are always harder on ourselves than others! Everyone makes mistakes; don't let your mistakes or your anxious feelings be an excuse to be unkind to yourself. For example, maybe you went to a social event but were only able to stay for a little while before your anxiety forced you to leave. You could engage in negative self-talk and criticize yourself for having to leave. Or you could be kind to yourself and remind yourself how hard it was to get there in the first place. Compliment yourself and appreciate your effort rather than tearing yourself down for your limitations.

Engage yourself in social situations in safe spaces: Work slowly from there. Seek out safe spaces and people to begin your journey. Maybe you have friends who also have anxiety or, at the very least, have understanding and patience. Ask them to go somewhere with you that feels easy – maybe a quiet coffee shop on a weekday morning, a park with lots of open space for people to spread out, or a small social gathering like a dinner or game night with just a few friends. As you begin to branch out and engage socially in small ways, you can slowly add people, places, and events into your life as you feel more comfortable. Your goal is to be able to go alone to public places and begin to converse with others as soon as possible.

Face your fears: Avoidance is not the answer. While you shouldn't rip off the band-aid and jump into a situation that you know will undoubtedly cause an anxiety attack, you should strive to keep moving forward and face your fears. You can't avoid society forever, and facing your fears can often make them less powerful and help you to overcome them. Ultimately, the sooner you take control of your life, the sooner you will enjoy the benefits of freedom from the effects of fear.

Talk to someone about your fears: Ideally, you'll have a professional in your corner who understands the causes, symptoms, and effective treatments of social anxiety and who you can talk to regularly. If not, seek a trusted friend or partner with whom you feel safe discussing your fears. If you have a partner, it can be helpful to express how you are feeling so that they understand your fear-based behaviors and can help you when you are overwhelmed. A friend, family member, or roommate can also serve in this role. Talking about your fears is one of the most important things you can do to help you overcome them. Sometimes, just saying your fear out loud is an effective way to eliminate its power.

Limit alcohol and substance use: Alcohol and substances can heighten your emotions, making your anxiety worse. Even if you feel they help to numb your anxiety, once they wear off, all those feelings will come right back, accompanied by feelings of guilt and shame. Also, using substances to help you deal with negative emotions can lead to overuse or, worse, addictive behavior, as each time, you'll need more to reproduce the same effect. Do yourself a favor; if you are in a fight to overcome social anxiety, avoid alcohol and substances until you feel confident enough to use them responsibly.

Take Massive Action:
Moderate Substances: Avoid comfort and coping mechanisms concerning social anxiety for one week. Face the discomfort head-on. Feel it, and let it wash over you, losing its power. For some, the coping may occur with the help of alcohol or painkillers. For others, it might be unhealthy foods or unhealthy quantities of food. For others, it may be shopping to feel the comfort of immediate gratification.

Navigating Social Situations with Ease... Even When You Feel Uneasy

At some point, a social event will come along that you will want to attend, even if you know that it will make you uncomfortable. Maybe your favorite charity is having a fundraiser that you'd really like to support, or even better, maybe your best friend is getting married on a riverboat and inviting 100 of their closest friends – including you! How fun! You know that you'd hate to miss either of those events, but going is more complicated than just making yourself get dressed and walking out the door. Suppose you want to navigate these types of situations successfully. In that case, you'll need to have some tools in your back pocket ready to use in times like these. Consider the following when you want to navigate a new social situation with ease:

Don't use substances to cope: We mentioned this above, but it's certainly worth reiterating; using a substance might seem like an easy way to get a bit of liquid strength, but in the long term, this is a dangerous strategy that can lead to a whole host of other problems. Therefore, it's probably best to avoid substances while you are working on your social anxiety coping skills.

Start small: Some people say, "Go big or go home," but that might not be the best strategy. You can undoubtedly go big when you feel ready, but it's better to start small with situations that only cause you a little anxiety and move up through the ranks to those situations that make you the most anxious.

Practice self-care: Anxiety can steal your energy. Make sure you practice self-care techniques to help you feel your best and make your potential social interactions more enjoyable. Plan out time before a social situation to relax—take a long hot shower, massage, mindful walk, or do something that you find relaxing and restful to be rested and ready to socialize.

Check-in with yourself: Checking in is as easy as recognizing your feelings. Ask yourself, what am I feeling right now? If you are anxious and need to center, try to elicit your senses. What do you see? What do you hear? What do you taste? What do you smell? What do you feel physically? This technique is critical and powerful. It can bring you back to reality, anchor your thoughts, and pull you out of the spiraling effects of a fight-or-flight reaction. When you are ready to refocus, remind yourself that this feeling of anxiety will pass.

Ask your support system for help: Many times, people with social anxiety suffer in silence while their loved ones want nothing more than to help. Communicate with those who love you how they can be most helpful and what they can do if they see you struggling with symptoms. Be direct and specific; most people will appreciate knowing exactly what you need so they can eliminate any guesswork. Taking a trusted and well-informed person with you to an anxiety-producing social situation can help you be more successful in navigating the experience.

Practice public speaking before going before a crowd: If you have to make a speech in public and don't know how to overcome your anxiety about it, consider practicing alone before going before the crowd. Practicing your speaking can be as easy as presenting to a small crowd of family and friends (or even pets!). You can even take this further and join an online speaking class or a group created for public speaking practices like Toastmasters. Never practice in front of a mirror. Your goal is to become less conscious of yourself. Mirrors accentuate your focus on you. Remind yourself that your focus is on adding value to others. You are presenting a gift, not going before a crowd for judgment.

Starting the Conversation...Tips for Talking to People

You've made it to the social event and want to try striking up a conversation with that attractive, interesting, irresistible person across the room. How do you begin, and how do you keep it going? Be bold and be the person to start. Before stepping out, quickly remind yourself that you are also attractive, interesting, and irresistible. I know that's incredibly terrifying, and you may not be able to identify with this truth at first. However, the person you want to speak with hopes to engage with attractive, interesting, and irresistible people. They might not know you are interested in a conversation. Be flexible; start with fun, encouraging small talk, and see where it leads. Once you are talking, be sure to be yourself. Most people are much more enjoyable when authentic and genuine interactions are more comfortable for everyone involved.

You can also ask questions to keep the conversation going. Just as most people usually think about themselves rather than the people around them, most prefer to talk about themselves. Showing authentic interest will make the person you are talking to feel comfortable to engage further in the conversation. Finally, make sure that you are being polite and respectful. Avoid talking too much or talking over others. Let everyone have a chance to speak, and when the conversation reaches its natural end, let the person know you enjoyed speaking with them or hope they have an excellent time at the social event.

In this chapter, we explored Social Anxiety and Social Anxiety Disorder. We discussed its causes, symptoms, and tips and strategies for overcoming it. As we move into the next chapter, we'll focus on boosting self-esteem and confidence—two critical social skills that can help you get out of your comfort zone and take you to the next level.

***

Ending With a Bang!

Take decisive action to gain the most impact on personal progress. Do the following as quickly as possible.

1. .**Reflect on Your Thoughts**: Each time a negative thought arises, write it down and critically assess its truthfulness.

2. **Shift Your Focus**: In your next social interaction, consciously focus on learning about the other person instead of how you're perceived.

3. **Emulate Confidence**: Act confidently in a situation where you usually feel anxious and reflect on the outcome.

4. **Ask Engaging Questions**: Prepare three questions to ask someone in a conversation to keep it flowing. Refrain from allowing these questions to distract you from actively listening to the other person, but lean on them if the conversation wanes.

Chapter 3
Building Your Strong Social Fortress... Without Putting Up Any Walls

Confidence is like a magnet that draws people towards you and helps to pave your way forward in many aspects of life. Of course, it also paves the way for you to approach others and talk to anyone! However, building and maintaining confidence can seem overwhelming - Especially when you struggle with self-doubt and negative self-talk! A surprising number of people struggle with confidence and something called "imposter syndrome."

Imposter syndrome is the feeling that you are not as skilled, talented, qualified, or good-looking as others may think you are. For example, let's say you land a great job. The imposter syndrome will make you feel like you shouldn't be there or aren't qualified to be there, and you are sure that eventually, someone will figure that out, and you'll be fired.

Even celebrities struggle with confidence or imposter syndrome. Prominent celebrities like Tom Hanks, Lady Gaga, and Maria Shriver have all discussed these same fears. Gina Vild, the author of the website Psychology Today, wrote about her experience with Imposter syndrome in the article "How I Cured Myself of Imposter Syndrome - Three Steps to Eliminate Fear of Being 'Too Much' and 'Not Enough.'" Gina was a young professional with a tremendous amount of potential. Yet, she was burdened by a nagging voice. A voice that told her she was an imposter. A feeling of inadequacy overshadowed every achievement she made, and every opportunity felt like a challenge she wasn't sure she was prepared to face.

It wasn't until she went on a date with a man she feared was way out of her league that she realized her inner turmoil may not accurately reflect how others see her. Sitting across from this man at dinner, whom she saw as sophisticated and accomplished, she thought surely this was a horrible mismatch, and he would eventually figure out how much better off he would be with someone else. So, she tried to beat him to the punch and began to offer to introduce him to her friend, who she thought would be a much better match. When he politely declined and instead told her all the many reasons why he was charmed by Gina, she had an epiphany - she needed to reshape her thoughts. From that day forward, Gina prioritized self-discovery and self-appreciation and began to try to shed the weight that imposter syndrome had put on her.

Over the years, Gina grew to higher and higher levels in her career while fighting her feelings of self-doubt. She learned to view her failures as stepping stones to growth and created a trusted circle of people who would give her honest feedback. Slowly, Gina exorcized imposter syndrome from her life and began to be able to offer her unique talents to the world with confidence and authenticity. Her story can give hope to anyone who is struggling with self-doubt. It's a great reminder that we should all embrace our strengths and share our true selves with those around us.

Find the Trend So You Can Confront It:
Reflect on situations where you feel like an imposter and write them down to recognize patterns.

Building and Maintaining Unshakeable Confidence

What is confidence anyway? And what does it mean to be confident? Confidence can be defined as a belief in yourself. This belief helps you to be self-assured and trust that you have the abilities and qualities to succeed. It is an inner strength that will lead you to pursue your goals, take risks, and face challenges that come up along the way. Very Well Mind (2024) notes, "It can refer to a general sense of trust in your ability to control your life, or it might be more situation-specific. For example, you might have high self-confidence in a particular area of expertise but feel less confident in others. In fact, research suggests that confidence is important to health and psychological well-being."

The benefits of building and maintaining your sense of confidence are nearly unending, and they compound over time. Being confident will help you to be more successful, and being more successful will help to build your confidence. Step by step, the benefits will roll in like a snowball going down a hill. As stated in the quote above, confidence can enhance your overall well-being. It does this by reducing your stress. A confident person will have a positive outlook, which can also improve your mental health and emotional stability.

Confidence can also help you be more assertive, improve your communication skills, and help you express yourself better at home and work. Also, when you can show your most confident self to the world, you are often perceived as more competent and trustworthy - this can open a world of opportunities. Very Well Mind (2024) says, "The doubt that comes with second-guessing yourself has internal and external repercussions. Confidence affects how you feel about yourself and communicates to others that you are trustworthy and capable - which can be helpful socially and at work."

With so many benefits to having confidence, it's essential to actively work towards building and maintaining it. You should take your time but work deliberately towards this goal, considering all the benefits you can expect!

Projecting Confidence

As you're working on building your confidence, recognize that you must feel it strongly. Did you know that you can put tools in your toolbox to help you project confidence to others even if you don't completely feel it on the inside yet? Projecting confidence can help to build your inner confidence! Projecting confidence is about presenting yourself in a way that inspires trust, respect, and credibility in others. This can be very beneficial because research has shown that confident people have more positive social interactions and are given more opportunities than those who do not appear to be confident. Someone who appears confident is more likely to succeed in their career, relationships, and everyday social situations. So, intentionally ensure your posture projects confidence. Take my story, for example.

For as long as I can remember, I have been shy. As a child, in public, I would nervously and unintentionally pull my shoulders up alongside my ears and hunch my head forward in a noticeably strange posture. Of course, this posture gathered other people's attention. And attention meant I would continue to become more self-conscious and perpetuate this nervous posture.

As a young teenager, I had to find a way to break the cycle. The more I focused on trying to posture myself "normally," or at least more like everyone else, I found that I would get caught up in my own thoughts of embarrassment and project that embarrassment in the form of more shy behavior and weak, vulnerable posture.

So, one day, I decided to stop trying to be "normal," instead, I chose to posture myself like a hero, like the most formidable and confident person in the room. I imagined that all my strength and potential were dangerous weapons and that if I weren't careful and focused on holding back, no one in the area would be safe. I was careful not to project a sense of violent intent but of overwhelming assurance. As a result, I stumbled into a method for projecting confidence, security, and capability.

Rather than seeing a shy and awkward teenager, people saw a confident, capable, and mature young person. My new powerful projection convinced others around me that I had become different, but something more significant was gradually happening. I began to feel confident and capable, which opened new doors for interacting with people in new ways. I started engaging in adult and teen conversations, relating to others of all ages as best as possible.

With time, I could dial back the somewhat childish position that I was a powerful and dangerous super-weapon. At some point, this projection faded away altogether. It was a necessary overcompensation, temporarily required to offset the intense feelings I constantly experienced of embarrassment, insignificance, and powerlessness.

The story's point: Don't aim for average if you feel intensely stuck. It may take intense expression, effort, or belief to break out and find your authentic state. It is also important to note that at that point in my life, I had not learned any conversational skills to change how I approached others. I simply changed my outlook about myself, which consequently changed how I approached people and opened doors of opportunity to talk to them.

Many factors play a role in projecting confidence to the outside world. Body language is one factor. It can significantly impact how people perceive you, especially during a first impression. Communication style and techniques are another major factor. Again, even if you don't feel it, acting like you do is a powerful tool. According to Speakers Institute (2024), "Researchers have found that the brain is capable of learning the new way of 'acting.' There's a reason why the phrase 'fake it 'til you make it' is still prevalent. You can train your brain to project confidence until it's second nature." Below is a list of techniques that you can use to help you use body language and effective communication to project confidence to those around you.

Below is a list of life-changing techniques that you can use to help you use body language and effective communication to project confidence to those around you.

Make good eye contact.

Good eye contact can speak volumes. It tells the person you talk with that you are sincere and confident while showing that you listen to what they say. They will simultaneously feel heard and engaged. Please don't stare at someone intensely, but look directly into their eyes while looking away occasionally.

Keep your chin up!

I'm sure you've heard from a parental figure about sitting up straight or not slouching sometime in your life! I heard it a lot as a kid because it was a bad habit of mine. However, to project confidence, you should hold your head high and avoid slouching or dropping your shoulders. Holding your head up shows confidence while also enhancing your facial features. People will look at you and think you are confident and approachable!

Lean forward

When talking to someone, lean slightly towards them. This body language shows that you are interested and want to participate actively in the conversation. Try not to lean back or cross your arms. This is subconsciously interpreted as anger or disinterest.

Avoid your pockets

Keep your hands out unless you need to reach for something in your pocket. Alanis Morrisette may have had one hand in her pocket, but you should try to have none! Instead, keep your arms relaxed or use your hands to help express yourself while speaking. This helps tell others that you are confident and open in your communication.

Don't fidget

Many of us struggle with being restless or sitting still, especially those with other challenges like ADHD. Sometimes, We don't even realize that we are fidgeting! Pay attention to your body to pinpoint times or circumstances that make you want to move more. Where are you when this happens? What time of day is it? What are you doing? Practice being still in quiet moments so that when you find yourself in the circumstances you were able to pinpoint, it will be easier to keep from fidgeting.

Take bigger, longer steps

Long, purposeful walking strides take up space and project confidence. Sometimes, people who struggle with confidence try to make themselves smaller so they can disappear into the background. You belong in this world and deserve to take up all the space you need! Take those big steps physically; they might even help you take them mentally.

Give a firm handshake

This sounds like old-fashioned advice (especially in a post-pandemic world), but a good firm handshake when greeting someone is one of the best ways to show that you are strong and assertive. A weak handshake is a quick and easy way for others to judge that you lack confidence. This is especially true in the business world. Try to give a firm grip (without being aggressive), make good eye contact while you shake, and don't forget to smile!

Mirror the body language of others

Mirroring involves paying attention to others' body language and subtly replicating their gestures and postures. This subconsciously creates a natural rapport with the person you are speaking to. They will feel connected and comfortable in your presence. They will see you as more confident and view the interaction as more positive.

Speak slowly and clearly

Speaking too fast will make you sound nervous. Slow down and speak at a steady pace. This will help others see you as both confident and knowledgeable. Along with a steady pace, you should also make sure you speak as clearly as possible and articulate your words coherently. If someone can't understand you, they won't be able to receive the message you are trying to convey. Slow down, take your time, and speak deliberately to project your confidence to others while speaking.

Loosen up your jaw and shoulders

You may already feel the tension in your shoulders, but did you know you can carry that same tension in your jaw? It's something that most of us don't feel unless we stop to notice it deliberately. Releasing the tension in your jaw and shoulders can help you seem relaxed and at ease with your circumstances. To help you do this, take a few deep breaths or use other relaxation techniques to loosen up your muscles and project confidence through your relaxed demeanor.

These body language techniques can enhance your communication style and improve your body language. Through these tips, you can project confidence in nearly any situation you find yourself in, and projecting confidence can improve how others see you. Even if you are not feeling entirely confident, you can boost your confidence by faking it until you make it and ensuring you get the attention and respect you deserve. Here are some more tips for projecting confidence in your daily life.

Improve your knowledge base in relevant areas.

Do you need more confidence at work or in social situations requiring more knowledge? One of the best ways to overcome this is to grow your knowledge base! Enhancing your expertise will make you feel confident in your knowledge and abilities.

Utilize assertive language.

Assertive communication is different from aggressive communication. Assertive communication involves expressing your thoughts, needs, and boundaries directly and respectfully. Practice speaking up for yourself and communicating to others what you need. This not only helps you feel confident but can also reduce your stress levels.

Know and uphold your values.

What do you believe in? What do you value? If you don't know, this is a great time to explore what you think about the world and what you hold dear. Knowing your beliefs and values gives you a touchstone to hold on to and can guide you throughout your life and decision-making. It builds the foundation for your behavior and fosters a sense of authenticity and confidence.

Own your expertise.

Think about what you already know—it is probably so much! Embrace your expertise and experiences with confidence. Recognize your unique skills, knowledge, and strengths, and be ready to communicate your expertise assertively to others. Most of us feel weird talking ourselves up, so don't be shy about confidently sharing your knowledge with others.

Dress in clothes that make you feel confident.

We all have that one outfit we put on, making us feel like a million bucks! What's yours? I feel particularly confident in boots – it doesn't matter if they are dress boots, hiking boots, or even combat boots (my favorite!); putting on a pair of boots with any outfit makes me ready to take on the world. Wearing clothing that makes you feel comfortable and empowered will boost your confidence and help you project confidence to the world.

> **Choose Your Exterior to Affect Your Interior:**
> **Enhance Your Appearance**: Dress in a way that makes you feel confident and powerful, impacting how you perceive yourself and how others see you.

Accept compliments.

Accepting compliments is hard, especially when you don't have enough confidence to feel you deserve them. For someone who lacks confidence, compliments can even feel embarrassing. When someone compliments you, they likely genuinely mean it and see something from an outsider's perspective that you can't quite see. Many of us are prone to denying compliments when they come our way; instead of denying them, try to accept them with confident grace. This will reflect a positive self-image and help your self-esteem to grow.

Additional Tactics

The tactics above will help you project confidence outwardly and take you far alone. However, please add the following steps to your arsenal to address your motivations and mindset. The below step-by-step process will help you boost your fortress of confidence beyond the power of outward projection alone.

Step 1: Take one step at a time.

It takes time, patience, and perseverance to build your confidence. Remind yourself that this is a process, and take it one step at a time. You can establish short-term goals to help you break the process down into small, more manageable tasks. Celebrate your victory when you accomplish a goal - no matter how small! Each goal will add to your overall progress and boost your confidence.

Step 2: Find your why.

What is your motivation for wanting to build your confidence? Do you want more career success? Or perhaps you want to be more social and have more friends? Your answer should reflect your values, passions, and aspirations. Understanding why your goals are meaningful can give you purpose and clarity, which can help you move forward toward the self-confident feeling you want. Psychology Today (2023) discusses the importance of knowing why when building confidence. They state, "What your why is, remind yourself of it because it will motivate you through any moments of doubt and make you even more passionate."

Step 3: Remember successes from your past.

Think of moments when you faced a challenge successfully or set a goal and met it. Thinking about times that you have been successful in the past can help reinforce your belief in what you can do in the present. If you are actively working to build your confidence, list times you have succeeded. Just like a scientist uses evidence to support their theories, you can use this evidence to support your ability to overcome obstacles and achieve your goals.

Step 4: Try out daily positive affirmations.

Sometimes, you must train your brain to help create a new habit or attitude. You can reprogram your brain and your mindset by practicing positive daily affirmations. An affirmation is a statement you can say out loud to yourself to reinforce positive beliefs about yourself and your abilities. There are positive affirmation daily calendars and even affirmation apps that can help you with ideas for positive affirmations. Here is a list of 20 to get you started in this daily practice.

- I can achieve anything I set my mind to.

- I am worthy of love and respect.

- I trust myself to make the right decisions.

- I know my abilities and talents will help me succeed.

- I can embrace challenges as learning opportunities.

- I am resilient, and I can overcome it.

- I deserve success and happiness.

- I believe in my potential.

- I exude confidence and positivity.

- I am enough.

- I deserve abundance and prosperity.

- I am surrounded by love and support.

- I attract positive people and experiences.

- I can face uncertainty with courage.

- I am unstoppable.

- I can let go of fear and trust the process.

- I am grateful for both my strengths and my weaknesses.

- I choose to let go of the past and focus on the present.

- I can create my own happiness.

- I believe in myself, even if I think others doubt me.

Step 5: Surround yourself with positive people!

When I was young, my mother used to tell me that it's much easier for someone to drag you down than for you to pull someone up. In other words, surrounding yourself with negative people will only bring down your confidence. A negative person might tell you that you can't do something or are not good enough. They may say they are just giving you helpful feedback, but good constructive feedback shouldn't be focused on something other than stopping you. Instead, it should be focused on helping you grow. If you fill your social circle with positive people who believe in your potential and desire to encourage your growth, they will help build your confidence and provide much-needed support. They will certainly give you feedback, but they will also help you see all that you are capable of!

Tips for Boosting Self-Esteem and Projecting Confidence

Self-esteem is vital in creating a positive self-image and building your social fortress. The Mayo Clinic (2024) notes, "Low self-esteem can affect nearly every aspect of life. It can impact your relationships, job, and health."

Self-esteem is your overall sense of worth and value. It is reflective of how you see and feel about yourself and can have a significant influence on your overall well-being, including on your thoughts and behaviors. Having good self-esteem will boost your confidence and your coping skills.

As you use strategies to boost your self-esteem, you will experience a boost in your ability to project confidence. Follow these steps to get started.

Step 1: Recognize what affects your self-esteem.

Reflect on the circumstances or experiences that make you feel inadequate. Ask yourself if these circumstances or experiences should have the right to hold you captive to inadequacy. By identifying these situations, you can be more aware of what influences your self-esteem and begin working on the truth that counteracts them.

Step 2: Be defiantly mindful of your thoughts and beliefs.

Earlier, we discussed the effect of inner dialogue on confidence. It can also influence self-esteem. Try to notice negative thought patterns or inner criticism and ask yourself why you think or feel that way. Question these thought patterns critically and with disdain. These thoughts are your enemy and do not deserve your respect. Bringing awareness helps you process them and change unhelpful thoughts or belief patterns.

Step 3: Adjust negative thoughts and beliefs.

Once you are mindful of your negative thoughts and beliefs, begin challenging them. You can challenge negative thought patterns or inner criticism through critical questioning. For example, let's say you are struggling to complete a task, and your negative self-talk tells you that you are a failure or ill-suited. You can ask yourself if this thought is a fact. What evidence do I have that this thought is true? What evidence do I have that it is false? Questioning your negative thoughts can shed light on reality and help you protect your self-esteem.

The Keys Overcoming Self-Doubt and Negative Self Talk

One major factor that influences our confidence, self-esteem, and self-assurance is our inner dialogue, which, when unmonitored, can descend into negative self-talk. This type of dialogue can become a harmful, repetitive pattern of thought that can undermine your self-worth. Three examples of negative self-talk include:

- **All-or-nothing thinking:** I failed or am failing this task, so I am a total failure.

- **Catastrophizing the negative:** I made a small mistake, and now everyone will think I'm stupid.

- **Personalizing:** I sent a message to my friend, and they have yet to respond. They must be mad at me, or worse – they no longer like me.

Don't let negative self-talk limit your potential or cause you to shrink back from learning to talk to others. There are decisive steps you can take to help you eliminate this dangerous pattern of thinking and rewire your inner dialogue to host a healthy mental environment where you can confidently enjoy sharing yourself with those around you.

Step 1: Challenge negative core beliefs.

If you can identify the core beliefs that lead to negative self-talk, you can begin challenging and eventually eliminating them. Question your negative core beliefs and try to replace them with more rational ones.

Step 2: Look for evidence of negative thoughts and beliefs.

Look at the evidence that supports negative thoughts and beliefs. When you scratch the surface, you will usually find that your negative self-talk is based on distorted thinking, not reality.

Step 3: Ask yourself if you're overthinking things.

Sometimes, we think too much! When you find your brain engaging in negative self-talk, ask yourself if what you are experiencing is an overreaction to your current situation. There might also be an alternative explanation that can help you find a more balanced perspective.

Step 4: Stop the thought.

When you are experiencing a negative thought pattern, stop it in its tracks! You can put the thought on pause and return later when you are in a better state of mind. Being mindful of your thought patterns and becoming more self-aware can help you catch yourself engaging in negative self-talk and redirect your focus to more positive thoughts.

Step 5: Reframe your thoughts to neutral or positive ones.

Once you stop your negative thoughts as they are happening, you can reframe or replace them with positive ones. It can help to plan! If you think about the typical negative self-talk that you struggle with, you can make a list of positive self-talk that you can use to combat it. Focus on reframing the situation more positively and creating solutions rather than dwelling on failures or shortcomings.

Step 6: Practice neutral or positive thinking as often as possible.

Use your reframed thoughts as daily affirmations to make them a habit. Practice being grateful for the little things and giving yourself compassion. This and mindfulness will help you have a more optimistic outlook.

Step 7: Don't view negative self-talk as a motivator.

While it may seem like you could use negative self-talk to motivate you to do better or be better, negative reinforcement is ineffective in motivating others or yourself. Don't use negative self-talk as a driving force; use positive thought and self-encouragement to help fuel your progress. Self-talk is a salesman, driving you to accept what it offers. If your self-talk is negative, shaming, or devaluing, you will never find the motivation to improve yourself. Instead, you will accept further what the thoughts offer.

Using these strategies and the steps discussed in this chapter, you can grow your confidence and self-esteem while eliminating negative self-talk and doubt. These are all powerful ways to increase your social skills and help you learn to talk to anyone! Remember that these strategies will take patience and perseverance, but overcoming your struggles with confidence will come with unlimited rewards and benefits.

Even More Strategies for Building your Social Fortress without Putting up Walls

But wait! There is more! Now that we have discussed some essential steps for building your confidence, we'll discuss some tips and strategies to help nurture and defend your confidence, giving you the tools to overcome internal resistance with resilience and positivity. The following list of mental shifts takes time to master. Remember that this is a journey, taking you ever closer to deeper relationships and the ability to enjoy opening yourself to others around you.

Forgive yourself.

Everyone makes mistakes. Dwelling on those mistakes or beating yourself up for them does not serve anyone well. It's okay to acknowledge when you have done something wrong, but don't let it set you back. Forgive yourself and move forward, embracing forgiveness to foster self-acceptance.

You are not your circumstances.

Don't let external factors like what you have achieved or what others expect determine your feelings about yourself. You have inherent value as a unique and wonderful human being. Don't let circumstances outside your control define your identity or how you see yourself.

See the positive.

Every day, we can choose to see the good in the world or the bad. Not everything is black and white, but most of the time, we can see our world from a positive perspective rather than a negative one. Every challenge is an opportunity to learn, grow, and overcome. Be grateful for who you are and appreciate even the smallest moments of joy. A change of perspective could change your whole day or world.

Build a support network.

Cultivate a community of like-minded individuals who will support and lift you when you feel down. These individuals will help affirm your worth, which, in turn, will help support your self-esteem. They will be encouraged during challenging times.

Take good care of yourself.

Prioritizing self-care can boost not only your physical well-being but also your mental and emotional well-being. Getting good sleep, eating healthy, nourishing foods, exercising regularly, and engaging in hobbies you enjoy can significantly impact your confidence and self-esteem.

Stop making comparisons.

Everyone is unique, and so is everyone's journey on this planet. Comparing yourself to other people doesn't do anyone any good. Focus on your progress and growth instead of creating arbitrary external standards based on how you perceive others' growth. Treat yourself like an individual and appreciate your progress.

Be kind, especially to yourself.

Think about the way you treat your friends or others that you love. You wouldn't shame them for a small mistake or failure. In the same way, you should not shame yourself! Treat yourself with the same compassion and understand that you would your best friend or partner. Acknowledge that making mistakes is just a factor of any growth process and that imperfection is a reality everyone must live with. You don't have to be perfect; just be you.

Practice positive self-talk.

Our internal dialogue can become harsh and damaging if we let it. Our greatest fears can become our worst critics in the deep recesses of our minds. But you can control your inner monologue and turn it into a positive and safe place if you work at it. Replace your self-doubt with some of those daily affirmations we discussed above to help you reinforce your worth and abilities. If you make a conscious effort, you can cultivate a better inner environment for your overall mental well-being.

Set achievable goals.

Break down larger goals into smaller, more manageable ones that you can work toward gradually. By making your goals more realistic and ensuring that they align with your overall values and aspirations, you can set yourself up for success. Every small victory will help equip you for more significant challenges in the future.

Engage in activities you enjoy, but don't avoid trying new things.

Activities that you already know you enjoy and are good at can positively affect your self-confidence if you engage in them regularly. However, you also shouldn't limit yourself to what is familiar. As you develop confidence, you should leave your comfort zone and experience new challenges. It's okay if you try something even if you find out you don't like it or aren't good at it - all you are doing is giving it a try. You never know; you may find out that you like it! Either way, it will foster a growth mindset that can expand your sense of self-confidence. That is ultimately the key to this principle: leave what is comfortable to become someone who copes well in the uncertain and unknown. It will teach you how to relax when delving into new territories and levels of conversation with others.

Practice healthy boundaries.

People who often struggle with self-confidence have trouble recognizing and asserting their own needs, preferences, and limits. This is where healthy boundaries come in. Boundaries can help protect your well-being and give you a good sense of self-respect. It means saying no to activities or relationships that will drain your energy or bring your confidence down while saying yes to activities and relationships that fill up your confidence tank. Maintaining your boundaries can empower you and give you a better sense of self-worth. If you struggle with boundaries, you should look deeper into any people-pleasing tendencies plaguing you. People-pleasing needs to be dealt with to properly own your position in conversations with others, regardless of their reaction to you or your stated position.

If you struggle with people-pleasing or boundaries, please find help and resources at https://posg.life/boundaries.

This chapter discussed building confidence and trust in yourself, established through consistency and practice. We embrace this by learning to let go of negative self-talk and see the reality of who we really are. In the upcoming chapter, we will transition into Part Two of this book, which teaches practical social skills development, refinement, and mastery. In this section, you will focus less on your underlying beliefs and more on crafting your conversational skills.

***

Ending With a Bang!

Seize the moment and take massive action to accelerate your personal progress. The key is to act swiftly and decisively on the following steps.

1. **Practice Positive Self-Talk**: Replace negative thoughts with positive affirmations each morning to cultivate a positive mindset.

2. **Engage in Self-Reflection**: Regularly reflect on your experiences and the lessons learned to deepen your self-understanding and confidence. Visit https://posg.life/FreeDCBE to download a free guided journal of **Daily Confidence-Building Exercises**. This journal currently sells on Amazon for $12.99

3. **Decide on your confident pose:** Perfect a posture that projects confidence, such as standing tall and maintaining eye contact. Practice your pose so that it becomes natural.

Part II: Developing Practical Social and Communication Skills
Chapters 4 – 6

"Effective communication is about more than just exchanging information. It's about understanding the emotion and intentions behind the information." — **Lawrence Robinson, Jeanne Segal, Melinda Smith, Effective Communication**

Chapter 4
Creating Your Social Masterpiece

G rowing up, Annalisa Barbieri, writer for the Guardian, was a silent observer of the conversations between her mother and their neighbor, Pam. Barbieri noticed a genuine need for more communication despite a constant exchange of words. Her mother and Pam would interrupt each other and interject their own anecdotes, but they never seemed to listen intently to each other. This experience inspired Barbieri to develop better communication skills throughout her life, and she worked hard to be a good listener.

When Barbieri took on the role of advice columnist for The Guardian, she realized the depth of understanding required in communication. She found that communicating isn't just about speaking and hearing words; it's also about understanding unspoken emotions and creating genuine connections. She aimed to hone her listening ability and to listen with her heart instead of her ears. As Barbieri did this, her interactions transformed, and she began to recognize that good communication is not in the exchange of words but in the depth of understanding and connection that the words foster.

Perhaps you think, "I don't like to talk to people; why do I need good conversation skills?" However, having good conversation skills can provide you with various benefits. To begin with, it helps establish meaningful connections. A good conversation can help you understand another person and help them to understand you. This mutual understanding can increase your empathy for others. Good conversation skills also help you share your ideas, perspectives, and experiences, which can lead to better relationships overall. Finally, it can provide you with professional benefits. Good conversation skills can help you communicate your knowledge or expertise in the workplace and enhance your work-life relationships.

This chapter will discuss how to start a conversation, organically turning small talk into deeper topics. It will provide tips for maintaining engaging conversations and turning casual interactions into lasting relationships. Many people think that communication skills are innate and that we are born with the ability to speak to others easily. However, that could not be further from the truth! Even if you are shy or socially anxious, you can build your communication skills, creating a social masterpiece to help you talk to anyone! So, let's dive in and discover multiple ways to improve our conversations and grow our communication skills.

How to Start Meaningful Conversations

Conversation happens so frequently throughout the day that we often don't give it much thought. However, most day-to-day conversations are relatively brief and can only sometimes be categorized as meaningful. Psyche (2024) defines meaningful conversation as "Conversation where we leave behind the shallows of small talk—however pleasant they might be—and dive deeper. These kinds of conversations are substantive; the key feature of deeper conversations is that you learn something." In other words, meaningful conversations take your connection with someone to another level.

Engaging in a more meaningful conversation can help you and the person you are talking to share thoughts, feelings, and experiences. This can lead to a deeper relationship and a sense of belonging. It will allow you to create a genuine connection. Meaningful conversations can also lead to having increased empathy - not only for the person you are talking to but also for others who share their characteristics. Finally, engaging in meaningful conversations can help create a positive and supportive environment where everyone feels comfortable expressing themselves and asking for input from others.

But what does a meaningful conversation look like? A meaningful conversation is characterized by open communication, active listening, and mutual respect. Those engaged in a deep and meaningful conversation will feel valued, heard, and encouraged to share their perspectives without fear of judgment. Meaningful conversations often involve discussing topics relevant and significant to everyone involved, leading to a deeper understanding of each other's thoughts and feelings. Now that we have defined a meaningful conversation, its benefits, and what it looks like, it's time to start improving your skills to make your conversations more profound. Below are some expert-level tips to prepare you for success on your journey:

Ask Open Questions

A simple yes or no cannot answer an open question and often begins with who, what, when, where, why, or how. By asking open questions, you invite others to share their thoughts, feelings, and experiences, fostering a more meaningful exchange of ideas. Rather than looking for concise answers, show your curiosity and sense of wonder toward your conversational partners. Allow them to feel that their stories matter and intrigue you. They will step out of chit-chat and into deeper connection as they perceive their answers as a fabulous scratch to a deep yearning in your curiosity.

Make Sure Everyone Gets a Chance to Share

Everyone involved in a conversation should have the opportunity to express themselves. To ensure everyone feels included, you must actively listen to each person, acknowledge others' input, and encourage anyone not participating to join. It would be best to create an inclusive environment so everyone feels valued and heard. If someone involved in the conversation seems quiet, tell them you are dying to listen to their thoughts. Be sure to compliment their ability to have such an exciting perspective whenever they share. Your positive and encouraging approach will charge the atmosphere with openness and anticipation for all involved.

Start Answers to Questions with the Phrase "For Me . . ."

Saying "for me" (or something similar) conveys that you are sharing a personal experience and indicates that you are speaking from your point of view. This also helps to show authenticity and helps encourage others to do the same. It allows space for other perspectives to coexist without a sense of rightness and wrongness that often divide people and stifle openness.

Respond to Others' Answers to Questions

If you ask someone a question, it is essential that you also listen and respond to their answer. When someone shares their thoughts with you, they share a part of themselves. Listening and responding to their response shows respect for their perspective, creating a more meaningful interaction.

Be Willing to Share Something about Yourself

Sharing something about yourself is an act of vulnerability. However, if you are with someone you trust, sharing an experience or your thoughts and feelings can invite them to do the same. Vulnerability creates intimacy, and people crave intimacy and connection.

The tips above are a great way to get you started; however, if you need more help, we have included:

Twenty great conversation starters for meaningful professional conversations.

1. What inspired you to pursue your current career?

2. What is your best problem-solving approach?

3. What challenges have you faced in your work recently?

4. What work project are you most proud of?

5. What motivates you to succeed?

6. What does your time management routine look like?

7. What is the best way to give constructive feedback?

8. What is one professional development goal you are working on?

9. What was the best team you have ever worked on?

10. How do you maintain a good work-life balance?

11. What is the number one quality someone needs in our industry?

12. What helps you to focus and be productive?

13. How do you find networking opportunities or building professional relationships?

14. What do you enjoy most about your job?

15. What is the best way to handle conflict in the workplace?

16. What leadership principle guides your decision-making?

17. What advice would you give someone who just started their career?

18. What would you choose if you had to choose another career?

19. What secret power or skill do you possess that few know about?

20. What industry will grow the most in the next ten years?

20 Conversation Starters for Personal Relationships, including Friends, Family, or Romantic Partners

1. What is your most cherished memory?

2. What's something that brings you joy?

3. What have you always wanted to try but have yet to?

4. What's your first childhood memory?

5. Are you an introvert, extrovert, or a combination of both?

6. What do you like most about yourself?

7. How have your priorities changed over the last five years?

8. Would you instead go into space or back in time?

9. What would be the title of your biography?

10. How do you overcome self-doubt?

11. What's one lesson failure has taught you?

12. What is your definition of respect?

13. What vacations did you go on as a child?

14. Who most influenced who you are today?

15. What is your definition of 'home'?

16. Would you rather be rich or intelligent?

17. When did you last feel proud of something you did?

18. What will society be like in 100 years?

19. What is your most unpopular opinion?

20. How do you define adventure?

Elevating Small Talk

"Small Talk" is those little everyday conversations about familiar topics like a recent local sports game or the weather. Small talk is not generally an intense conversation. However, these types of conversations can be a gateway to more meaningful connections and richer conversations if you know how to elevate them. Small talk can help you establish rapport with another person and build your relationship over time. It creates a comfortable space that you can use to gain deeper insight into the other person's likes, dislikes, and feelings.

One strategy for elevating small talk is called 'vertical questioning.' Psychology Today describes this strategy as follows: "Vertical questioning prods the person you're conversing with to turn inward and think about their response more profoundly. Vertical questioning is the key to making small talk or casual conversation much more interesting and satisfying—for you and the other person. This conversational technique creates an environment of curiosity and understanding."

To ask vertical questions, you need to ensure your questions are open-ended. A horizontal question gathers facts, while a vertical question gathers the information behind the facts, like emotions, values, and experiences. You can begin with a horizontal question like, "Where did you go on your trip?" Then, after you find out they went on a cruise, turn it into a vertical question as a follow-up asking, "Which excursions did you enjoy most?"

Vertical questioning is just one of many techniques for elevating small talk. Below are more action items for moving from small talk to more extensive and deeper conversations.

Have a variety of small talk openers at your disposal, and use the best one for the situation.

Preparing for your conversations is a great strategy; having mental notes for general conversation starters for new people can help, too! Pull from the environment around you. For example, comment on the muffins at a meet-and-greet or a display at a networking event and ask what others think about them.

> **Take Action to Grow:**
> **Prepare Conversation Starters**: Prepare a list of engaging topics or questions to help initiate and sustain conversations in any setting.

Ask questions that spark joy.

Asking questions that help remind others of positive experiences or emotions can get the conversation going. Asking about someone's passions or hobbies is one way to start. Also, any question about someone's favorite part of something or best experience will spark joy and inspire lively conversation.

Have some stories ready and invite others to share theirs.

As soon as our ancient ancestors began gathering around a fire at the end of a long day, story-telling was present to engage and connect with others. However, if you struggle to speak to others, consider what stories you could tell beforehand. What's the most exciting thing that has ever happened to you? For example, when I was four years old, I met Mohammed Ali in an elevator, and he asked me for a bite of my cookie. I dared to tell him, 'No way!" In just two sentences, I told you an exciting story that can help inspire others to tell stories about times when they met a celebrity. Stories should be brief but also compelling. For every experience you share, remember to invite others to share a story about their own experiences.

Utilize topics you have in common with the other person.

What common interests do you share with the other person? Try to hit on those topics so that you can use your shared experience to discuss things further. If you cannot arrive at a common interest, open-handedly explain why you hold your position. Then, ask what others might recommend to help you see their interest in another light.

Be honest.

Authenticity is an essential factor in creating a meaningful connection. Being genuine is not just about avoiding bold lies (though that is also important!) but also about showing your true self to others. You should be open while encouraging the other person to do the same. Some might even argue that you can't be genuinely connected with another person unless you are vulnerable, which involves an honest approach to your interactions.

Using these action items, you can turn your everyday small talk into meaningful conversations and create deeper connections with others. This transition from small talk to "deep talk" allows for exploring more profound thoughts, feelings, and experiences, fostering a deeper connection and sense of empathy between individuals. As a result, you cultivate stronger relationships and gain deeper insights into the perspectives and inner worlds of those around you.

Turning Dialogue Into a Rich and Engaging Experience for Everyone

In this chapter, you have learned how to begin a conversation and take that conversation from small talk to something more profound. But once you start a conversation, how do you keep it going? Keeping a conversation flowing is a crucial part of good conversation skills. Below, you will find some detailed tips on maintaining an engaging discussion.

Practice.

How do you improve a skill? Did you say "practice"? Correct! Conversation skills are like any other; they require practice to hone. You have to get out there and do it to practice conversation skills. Try engaging in regular conversations with different people to help improve your skills and build your confidence.

Be genuinely interested.

Show genuine curiosity and interest in the other person's stories, experiences, and perspectives. Active listening and genuine engagement enhance the quality of the conversation and strengthen the connection between participants. Others will see in your eyes and expression if you are genuinely engaged and interested in them.

Refrain from filling the silence during pauses.

This one is TOUGH for me! Allowing natural pauses in a conversation enables your brain to process the information you just listened to and formulate the next thought. It also creates space for others to join in and take their turn speaking. If the pause goes on for too long and gets awkward, you can ask another question to get it going again, but be bold and leave a few seconds of silence for others. Another tactic, if the silence becomes awkward, is to say something fun like, "What an awkward silence we just created together." Laughing and using inclusive terms can take the edge off of awkwardness.

Ask follow-up questions.

Follow-up questions show genuine interest in what the other person is saying. This can be as simple as saying, "I'd love to hear more about that." Or asking, "How did that make you feel?" Follow-up questions can deepen the conversation and encourage further discussion. Remember to keep the conversation open with a simple yes or no comment that leaves little for the other person to respond to.

Give compliments.

A sincere compliment about someone's achievements, contributions, or positive personal traits can help to create a better rapport. Avoiding complimenting something superficial like, "Lovely blouse!" or asking, "Have you lost weight?" These compliments or questions generally won't lead to better conversation. Instead, you can say something like, "Congratulations on receiving the quarterly award! What's your next goal?"

Bring up appropriate current events.

Current events can be a great topic of conversation, but you should avoid discussing controversial issues, especially with people you don't know very well. Politics, religion, personal health, or income are some of the major topics you should avoid. Be mindful of what your conversation partner is sensitive to and tailor your conversation around those sensitivities.

Be careful about making jokes that could be viewed as offensive or insensitive.

Along with being sensitive to current events, make sure that the jokes you tell are not offending others under the guise of humor. Humor can be a great tool in your conversation toolbox, but you must consider the context and impact of your jokes. If you think your joke might offend someone, it's usually best to avoid it.

Avoid making judgments.

We could all improve the tendency to judge people too quickly and from a distance! Making assumptions about another person can prevent you from engaging in meaningful relationships. Approach conversations with an open mind and willingness to listen and learn from the other person without judgment.

Balance asking questions and sharing information.

Aim for a 50/50 balance of asking questions and sharing information. Too many questions can make your conversation partner feel on trial! However, sharing too much information without asking questions can make your conversation partner feel bored. They might conclude that you are uninterested or only wish to talk about yourself.

> **Listen As Much as You Speak**: Focus on listening actively to truly understand and connect with the speaker rather than waiting for your turn to talk.

Avoid checking your phone.

If you truly want a deeper and more meaningful conversation, give it your full attention. Try to minimize distractions by putting your phone on silent or putting it away where you cannot see it. This goes for other technology, too, like tablets or even TV. Turn off technology so you can focus on your conversation partner with intention.

Avoid gossip.

Gossip may be fun, but sharing gossip with others can make them feel like you are not trustworthy. If you are gossiping about someone else, what will stop you from gossiping about them? Stay away from gossip or negative talk about others. This type of conversation can damage relationships. Instead, focus on positive topics that will leave all participants better off at the end of the conversation.

Know when to end the conversation.

Have you ever been conversing with someone you thought would never end? Was that a fun conversation to be in? Probably not! Pay attention to social cues that indicate that a conversation has reached its end or that it is time to move on to speak with someone else. The other person may have looked at their watch, looked away, or perhaps another person is approaching. If you end a conversation politely, it shows respect for the other person and leaves a positive impression after the interaction. Be sure to thank the other person for the wonderful discussion. If you want to be memorable as you depart, consider looking back and flashing a smile of gratitude to leave a more lasting impression of connection in the other person's mind.

Turning Casual Interactions Into Meaningful Connections

The tips presented in this chapter help turn casual interactions into meaningful connections. Putting these tools in your social toolbox can help you to have conversations that build better relationships. Practicing active listening, asking open-ended questions, and sharing personal experiences with others can help you engage more deeply and empathize. We all want more meaningful and authentic relationships; engaging in deeper conversations can help us get them! Consider these final tips as a cheat sheet concerning the overall flow of discussions:

• Begin with Small Talk: Begin with small talk and use vertical questions to elevate! Or, keep initial conversations and build up for longer.

• Have a Positive Mindset: You are interesting to talk to and worthy of attention. Go into conversations with a positive mindset and assume good intentions.

• Keep it Moving (Even when it gets awkward): Don't let one awkward moment or silence ruin your conversation. Push through, ask an additional question, be charming, laugh, or offer an interesting anecdote to move the conversation forward.

• Aim for Vulnerability and Authenticity: Be open and honest. Embrace what is unique about yourself and others. Being vulnerable helps your conversation partner do the same and builds trust.

• Encourage Them to Share: Encourage deeper conversations by asking questions and listening to the responses. Invite others to share their thoughts and feelings and respect their responses.

• Respect Boundaries: We all have boundaries; try to recognize and honor the boundaries of others. This includes respecting their privacy, comfort levels, and personal space.

• Be Intentionally Engaged: Be present in the conversation. Avoid distractions and give your conversation partner your full attention. You can't form meaningful connections while distracted.

Henry had always struggled with engaging in meaningful conversations. During one memorable encounter, he asked a new acquaintance the same question twice, not because he forgot the answer but because his nerves had prevented him from listening well in the first place. The redundancy created a palpable awkwardness, causing the conversation to fizzle out. Mortified, Henry replayed the scenario in his head for days, berating himself for the blunder.

Determined to learn from his mistake, Henry realized he needed to focus more on listening actively than on methods for trying to impress. This shift in approach proved transformative. His subsequent conversations flowed more naturally, and he exuded newfound confidence. One evening, at a networking event, he found himself engrossed in a discussion with a fascinating person who hinted at an exciting opportunity. As they delved deeper, would Henry continue to actively listen or be distracted by his desire to win the opportunity?

This chapter has focused on the art of having a good conversation. We briefly touched on the role of listening; in the next chapter, we will discuss active listening in greater practice and how to add that tool to your social toolbox. Being able to talk to anyone also means listening to anyone. Tune in to the next chapter to learn how.

Ending With a Bang!

Adopt a strong commitment to applying the following strategies as quickly as possible to ignite rapid personal growth.

1. **Give Compliments**: To build positivity and rapport, offer genuine praise to others about their ideas, achievements, or qualities—practice by giving three people genuine praise every day for a week.

2. **Practice Intently**: Dedicate daily time to practice your conversation skills with friends, family, or even strangers to build confidence. Practice active listening, asking deeper questions, sharing personal insight, and responding intently to the other person's words.

3. **Respond Thoughtfully**: Show genuine interest in others' replies by listening carefully and responding thoughtfully to deepen the connection. Hold one conversation daily this week where you share your thought only after you have acknowledged and spoken to the last thing the other person shared in the conversation.

Chapter 5
Discovering the Super Power of Active Listening

Have you ever been in a conversation with someone and left never truly feeling heard? The other person may have interrupted and inserted their thoughts or ideas before you could communicate your own. Or perhaps the other person changed the subject before you felt like you had finished sharing your thoughts. Are you likely guilty of these things yourself? These actions indicate that someone is having a problem listening actively.

What is Active Listening . . . and Why is it Crucial?

Active listening is a powerful social tool that goes so beyond just hearing the words that another person is saying. When you listen actively, you are fully engaged in a conversation. Through this engagement, you demonstrate a genuine interest in the other person and understand what they are trying to say. This communication technique provides constant feedback to the speaker, which helps them feel both heard and understood. When actively listening, you also go beyond spoken words and understand the context, emotions, and intentions communicated through nonverbals like tone and body language.

Active listening can help you establish meaningful relationships through effective communication. According to the Cleveland Clinic (2023), "Teachers, therapists, and barbers need to be able to engage with and really hear other people all day, every day, as part of their jobs. But everybody needs these skills.

Active listening was instrumental in improving the climate of my marriage. I was more of the guilty party but hadn't realized it yet. Struggling, we reached the end of our rope and found a marriage counselor to help us get past our sticking point.

He helped me to understand and practice the art of active listening. At first, the process was awkward and cumbersome. It made conversations feel twice as difficult. I had to pause my thoughts, listen, and respond well, yet that practice competed with my overly active desire to share what I actually wanted to say. I felt like my brain was overloaded.

To this day, I have to fight the desire to be heard and understood. It is more important that I listen and respond to the other person. If there is time to share my thoughts, that is a bonus. If not, I can initiate another conversation when there is more time. Very little in life is so urgent that it requires immediate communication. You may need help to accept this fact if you have an overactive mind. You may need a counselor like I did. Your spouse may thank you for seeking help.

Why should you care? Whether you're navigating work, family, romantic or other personal relationships, being good at actively listening to others has many benefits." Here are just a few of those benefits:

Improves Empathy: When listening actively, you are more likely to understand your conversation partner's emotions and points of view. Doing this can help you put yourself in the other person's shoes, strengthening your ability to empathize and connect on a deeper level.

Builds Mutual Trust: This is especially true when an uneven power dynamic exists. Employees who feel their boss hears them will be more likely to trust them. It creates a sense of rapport, forming the foundation for a better relationship.

Demonstrates Respect: By acknowledging another's thoughts and feelings without judgment or interruption, we demonstrate respect and help them to feel validated. This can build others' self-confidence and help them to understand healthy boundaries.

Diffuses Conflict: In my experience, often, the only thing that an angry or upset person wants is just to feel heard. Active listening can help de-escalate conflict, reduce tension, and create an environment of understanding and open communication.

Makes you a powerful ally: When we actively listen, we allow the other person to process their feelings. They find a resolution to a problem or hurt as they process. They may even find a new perspective they hadn't considered developing as they process. Whatever the outcome, you get to be a part of their small victory, making you a powerful ally in their experience.

Elements of Active Listening

To successfully actively listen, you must be "active"! There are elements that you can employ to help you to take action while you listen. Here are a few to consider:

Being fully present:

Active listening requires you to give your full attention without distraction to concentrate on what is being said. This means tuning in and listening with all your senses. Very Well Mind (2024) says, "Being fully present involves the skill of tuning into the other person's inner world while stepping away from your own." Stop planning what you are going to say next.

Paying attention to body language:

You can use non-verbal communication to listen beyond your conversation partners' words and understand their feelings. Alternatively, you can communicate to them through your nonverbal cues that you are listening intently by smiling, leaning in, and nodding when appropriate.

Making eye contact:

Good eye contact can communicate that you are present and listening to what your conversation partner is saying. This will show that you are attentive and interested in the conversation. Very Well Mind (2024) notes, "At the same time, you don't want to use so much contact that the conversation feels weird. To avoid this, follow the 50/70 rule - maintaining eye contact for 50% to 70% of the time and only holding for four to five seconds before looking away."

Asking open-ended questions:

In the last chapter, we discussed how to ask good questions to help create a meaningful conversation. This is also relevant to active listening. Avoiding the "yes or no" type and asking more open-ended questions will show that you are interested in learning more about the person you are speaking with.

Reflecting what you hear:

This element of active listening involves paraphrasing or summarizing what the other person has said and repeating it to them. This confirms to the speaker that you have understood what they have said and shows that you are actively engaged in the conversation. The speaker can then confirm if you have accurately captured their message and add clarification if necessary.

Time to Practice:
Reflect and Paraphrase: In your next conversation, practice summarizing the other person's words to ensure understanding. Pause and wait for them to confirm or clarify your summary before you reply.

Being patient:

It can be challenging to let another person speak without interrupting them. However, actively listening means allowing another person to talk freely. Refrain from filling silences with your own stories or thoughts, and as said before, don't spend time when you should be listening by preparing what you will say next.

Refraining from judgment:

Prematurely evaluating another person's thoughts can halt open communication before it even starts. Remaining neutral will create a safe zone where they can communicate freely without negative implications.

An Example of Active Listening

We've now discussed some of the significant elements of active listening, but what does this look like in a conversation? Here is an example of a conversation where active listening techniques are employed well.

Colleen: You'll never believe the night I had. I had a massive fight with my sister; now, she's not speaking to me. I'm so upset and don't know who to talk to.

Tony: Well, you can certainly talk to me; tell me more about what happened. (Open-Ended Question)

Colleen: It's so silly; it all started with an argument about our parents' anniversary party. She wants a big, expensive party, which I can't afford. She didn't want to see my perspective at all!

Tony: That sounds tough. (Empathizing) It sounds like you are upset that she wasn't seeing your point of view. (Reflecting)

Colleen: Exactly! I also feel guilty because my parents deserve a great party, and I hold everything back. I told her to go ahead and do it without me, but I don't feel good about that either.

Tony: I can understand why you would have such complicated feelings. (Empathizing) Sounds like you'll need some time to process all of this. (Withholding Judgement)

Colleen: Definitely, thank you so much for listening; I needed to vent!

How Relationships Benefit from Active Listening

Empathy and understanding another person's viewpoint are essential in any relationship. Understanding that you are not the only participant in a conversation can help you be more empathetic and create a better connection. Here's a breakdown of how active listening can benefit different relationships.

Personal relationships:

Active listening can help your friends and family feel that they have a safe space to share their thoughts and feelings with you. Very Well Mind (2024) mentions, "Active listening helps you better understand another person's point of view and respond with empathy. This is important in all types of healthy relationships, whether with a spouse, parent, child, another family member, or friend."

Romantic relationships:

Active listening can reduce misunderstandings and enhance good communication. It builds trust and encourages more profound relationships and open communication, leading to a more meaningful relationship with your romantic partner.

Professional relationships:

Active listening isn't just a good skill for romantic or personal relationships; it can also improve workplace communication. You can build better teams, enhance relationships between employees and managers, and create a more collaborative work environment through active listening.

New relationships:

At the beginning of any relationship, you must build a good foundation to determine how you will communicate. Whether it is a new friendship, professional relationship, or romantic partner, the connection you form early on through active listening will create trust and build a better relationship overall.

How to be an Active Listener:

Anyone can develop active listening skills; it just takes time and practice. We have walked through the concepts earlier in this chapter. Below, I will translate these concepts into action steps to enhance your active listening skills.

Providing undivided attention: Put away your phone and eliminate other distractions that can help you give all of your attention to the conversation. This will help you listen actively and show respect for the speaker.

Use expressions and body language that show interest: You can show your interest nonverbally through your facial expressions and nonverbals. Lean in, make good eye contact, and smile when appropriate to show that you are actively listening.

Restating information: Repeat pieces of the conversation or information that show someone you have listened to what they said and are engaged in the conversation.

Summarizing information: After someone tells you a story, give a one-sentence summary to show your understanding and empathy.

Using minimal encouragers: You can say or do a minimal encourager to encourage the speaker without inserting too much into the conversation. It can include nonverbal or verbal reactions like, "mmhmm," "really," or "I see."

Reflecting on conversations: Reflect on the speaker's feelings or intentions to show you understand the speaker's perspective. You could say, "I can see that really upset you." Or, "It sounds like that was really tough."

Asking helpful questions: Asking open-ended and reflective questions that help the speaker elaborate and share further can enhance your active listening.

Request Clarifications: In your next conversation, commit to ask clarifying questions to deepen your understanding of the speaker's point of view before you make your response. No matter how unnatural this may feel, tell yourself that you are not allowed to respond until you ask for clarification first.

Naming core emotions: By helping the speaker name an emotion, you can better empathize with them, validate their feelings, and help them process their emotions. You could simply say, "You sound sad." Or, "I hear you expressing some anger."

Using "I" statements: Your statements like, "You should . . ." can make them feel judged, which can close down communication. Turning your statements into "I" statements like, "I would feel angry if that happened to me." Or, "I feel concerned when you say that."

Providing feedback: You can ask if the speaker is open to feedback; if they are, you can share your observations of the situation. If they respond that they don't want feedback, let them move the conversation forward and continue your role as the listener.

Avoiding conversation dead ends: Dismissing someone's feelings, interrupting, offering unsolicited feedback, becoming distracted by your phone, asking judgemental questions, or somehow turning the focus back on you and away from the speaker are all ways to bring the conversation to a quick dead end.

Getting clarification when needed: Periodically ask for clarification or additional information when you need it to help create mutual understanding and show that you care about the speaker's message.

Recalling previously shared information: When appropriate, refer back to prior parts of the conversation, citing specific details. This shows that you have been listening attentively and helps to create a mutual understanding of the speaker's intent.

Mastering the art of active listening is not just a good skill to have; it's a social skill superpower that can help you show your empathy, respect, and interest in the speaker. Becoming a master of active listening can help you have more meaningful relationships and talk to anyone!

Conclusion:

In this chapter, we discussed the importance of active listening. Active listening is your social skills superpower that can help you engage in meaningful ways and help the people you speak with feel genuinely valued and heard by you. This creates an environment of understanding where others feel safe and trust you as a friend with whom they can share their thoughts and feelings. We also explored techniques and strategies to help you improve these skills and easily navigate a conversation with anyone!

The next chapter will analyze the elements of non-verbal communication and help you understand facial expressions, body language, gestures, and tone to understand and use non-verbal communication effectively.

These techniques can help you have better, deeper, and more meaningful relationships with others and enrich your social life and interactions.

***

Ending With a Bang!

Seize the moment and take decisive action to accelerate your personal progress. Swiftly implement the following steps to maximize your growth.

1. **Make active listening a priority in your daily life:** Log your daily conversations for a week, noting moments when you truly engaged in active listening versus when you didn't. Reflect on what triggered each type of response, making you feel more connected and valued in your interactions.

2. **Reflect and Paraphrase**: Pair up with a colleague or friend and take turns speaking for one minute, then paraphrasing each other's statements.

3. **Validate Feelings**: Practice sessions with friends where you focus solely on validating their feelings without offering solutions.

4. **Learn from Each Interaction**: Keep a reflective journal of your conversations, focusing on what went well and what could be improved.

Chapter 6
The Key to Understanding Non-Verbal Communication

Genuine communication is multilayered. While the most apparent aspect of communication is the words people say, there are more subtle but still powerful signals we convey through nonverbal cues. Sometimes, these nonverbal cues communicate more than our words. Our body language, tone, gestures, and facial expressions can help us better connect with those we speak to. Alternatively, they can work against us and build barriers even if we don't intend to - or even if we don't know it's happening!

Ruth H. Nobile, a Chemist for Bayer Pharmaceuticals and Professor of Pharmacy at Rutgers University, gives a personal example of learning about the importance of non-verbal communication in her article "The Power of Nonverbal Communication: Saying Everything Without Saying Anything." She discusses an experience that she had leading her very first team meeting. She spent many hours getting ready. She wanted to be confident about what she communicated and know the information well enough to answer any question. She studied and practiced until she felt ready to share her prepared information confidently.

Everything changed, however, when she walked into the room. Once she was looking at everyone she was supposed to be communicating with, her confidence began to wane. Nobile (2024) says, "My body language started to change: I stopped smiling, my shoulders started to sink, and even the tone of my voice was off. I was quickly losing the focus of people in the room, as my lack of self-confidence caused them to lose confidence in me." As the meeting went on, Nobile realized her nonverbal effect on the meeting and began to overcome it. She stood up straight, smiled, and refocused her thoughts to regain her confidence. By the end of the meeting, she had won back the room and maintained the team's attention. She notes that no matter the situation, your knowledge of the topic, or your level of expertise, you need to communicate the message confidently to communicate effectively.

In this chapter, we will explain how to analyze the elements of non-verbal communication so that you can read between the lines while listening to others speak. We'll also discuss how to communicate effectively non-verbally to help you show more confidence and make your message more compelling through your facial expressions, body language, gestures, and vocal tone. All these new tools will help you improve your communication skills and, as always, make talking to anyone easier and more enjoyable.

What is Non-Verbal Communication?

Non-verbal communication describes the messages we communicate to others without using words. This could involve communicating through facial expressions, gestures, or even body posture. Very Well Mind (2024) says, "A substantial portion of our communication is nonverbal. Some researchers suggest that the percentage of nonverbal communication is four times that of verbal communication, with 80% of what we communicate involving our actions and gestures versus only 20% being conveyed with the use of words." Did you catch that? A whopping 80% of your communication may come from every part of you except your words. Perhaps I should have changed the title of this book to **How To Communicate to Anyone Nonverbally.**

Let's look at a list of the primary elements of nonverbal communication.

Elements of non-verbal communication

Facial expressions

Every feeling or emotion can usually be read on our faces! Our faces tell the world how we feel, from joy to anger or surprise to sadness. There are even facial movements called microexpressions, which only last less than a second and can reveal our true feelings even if we are trying to hide them.

Gestures

The movements of our hands, arms, and body while speaking to add depth or clarity are called gestures. We can use gestures to our advantage to emphasize a point, provide clarification, or even substitute words entirely. Gestures, including nodding, waving, giving a thumbs up, and much more!

Paralinguistics (vocal tone)

The tone, speed, and rhythm of voices can communicate messages beyond words. Speaking too fast or with a broken rhythm can communicate nervousness, while speaking too slow might communicate confusion. The tone of our voices can reassure or warn.

Body language and posture

How we hold or position our bodies can send positive and negative information to others. Leaning forward can communicate that you are interested in a conversation while leaning back with your arms folded can communicate that you are closed off to the conversation or uncomfortable with the person you are speaking to.

Nonverbal communication can significantly impact verbal communication non. No matter what words are coming out of your mouth, your nonverbal cues will enhance them in positive ways or contradict them in negative ones. Your nonverbal cues will determine how your words are interpreted or understood. Without being aware of what nonverbal messages you are communicating and being able to interpret the nonverbal messages of others, you are only giving or receiving half of the message. Learning nonverbal language will help you communicate at a higher level.

Think about the last time you met someone new. Whether you were introduced at a party or other social situation or you met while going about your everyday activities, meeting someone new can be overwhelming, and often, judgments are made quickly on first impressions.

Suppose you were fidgeting, frowning, avoiding eye contact, crossing your arms, and leaning away. In that case, your potential new friend might have thought you were disinterested in the conversation. However, if you were smiling, maintaining good eye contact, and leaning in when they were speaking, they would have more likely interpreted you as interested and engaged. These nonverbal messages would have had a powerful impact on the situation's outcome.

Being able to read and give off non-verbal communication accurately is crucial. Whether in the boardroom, classroom, or social setting, mastering the silent language enables individuals to forge meaningful connections, build trust, and confidently navigate the complexities of human interaction. Nonverbal communication can serve a role in strengthening relationships as it fosters closeness and intimacy in interpersonal relationships. It can also be a substitute for spoken words, signaling information that a person might not want to or be able to say out loud. It reinforces the meaning of our words and can also help regulate the flow of a conversation by indicating the start and end of a message or topic.

Decoding Facial Expressions

Accurately reading facial expressions is a crucial part of understanding nonverbal communication. We can hide a lot within our communication, but hiding our face is difficult or near impossible. Very Well Mind (2024) notes, "The ability to understand facial expressions is important to nonverbal communication. If you only listen to what a person says and ignore what their face is telling you, then you really won't get the whole story. Often, words do not match emotions, and the face betrays what a person is actually feeling."

One fascinating example is called "duping delight." Duping Delight is when a person lying gives glimpses of a slight smile or smirk. Their brain is delighted that it is getting away with something, even something small, and they will unconsciously give themselves away with this expression.

Decoding facial expressions involves recognizing subtle cues and patterns associated with the emotions they reflect. While cultural norms and individual differences can influence facial expressions, certain emotions are universally recognized and expressed.

A friend of mine spent a week in Paris, the first time he had been to Europe. He walked the streets, 16 and innocent, smiling broadly and making eye contact with everyone in his path. However, he soon came to find quite a bit of unwanted attention. He didn't know his facial expression told the local French he was interested and available in their romantic intentions.

Many researchers have studied how different cultures interpret emotions. Psychology Today (2016) notes, "Despite the universality of basic emotions, as well as the similar facial muscles and neural architecture responsible for emotional expression, people are usually more accurate when judging facial expressions from their own culture than those from others." Therefore, be patient and straightforward when communicating with someone from another culture. It would be best to avoid sarcasm because other cultures might not read your face and take your statement seriously. Ask for clarification if you don't understand the speaker's message, and provide clarity for the listener as needed.

Understanding Body Language and Gestures

Body language and gestures are the next tools you can include in your nonverbal communication toolkit. Like facial expressions, reading these silent signals can enhance your communication skills and create better and stronger relationships. According to PsychCentral (2021), "At the most basic level, body language is an external signal of a person's inner emotional state. Body language is the story our bodies tell about how we think and feel." Intentional body language is relatively easy to understand, like a thumbs up when you've done something right or a stamped foot when someone is angry. However, unintentional body language can require more effort to interpret.

Interpreting the silent signals of body language can have many benefits. First, understanding body language can give you the key to understanding any communication more deeply. You may be missing part of the message if you don't know what someone's body is trying to say to help their mouth communicate. Understanding nonverbal cues through body language can also help you further your perception of their underlying emotions. This can help you empathize with others' experiences and foster better connections. Finally, understanding body language can help enhance your persuasive skills, help you appear more confident, and navigate social situations more easily.

Eye contact is vital in nonverbal communication and what your nonverbals communicate. It can convey to others that you are paying attention, interested, and engaged. On the other hand, avoiding eye contact can show discomfort and shyness or make the listener feel that you are trying to hide something from them. Good eye contact helps establish trust, which is particularly important early in new relationships. It also creates more connection with those with whom you already have a relationship and creates a sense of openness between two people.

Posture is another crucial factor in mastering nonverbal communication. Your posture can community confidence, level of authority, and attitude in a given situation. Straight and upright postures communicate that you are self-assured and confident about the topic you are speaking on. On the other hand, if you slouch or hunch over, you communicate the opposite message. This says to the other person that you are insecure, bored, or not engaged in the conversation. Paying attention to your posture can create a more favorable impression and show confidence in social settings.

Eye contact and body posture are just a few aspects of body language you should be aware of. Work on using yours appropriately as you prepare to talk to anyone. Below is a list of some of the other elements and how to analyze each.

Take Action:
Mirror a Conversation Partner: Pair up with a partner and engage in a conversation. Deliberately mirror your partner's body language, then switch roles. Afterward, discuss how mirroring affected your feelings of connection and understanding.

How to Read Body Language

Smiles and mouth expressions

A genuine smile can be seen both in the eyes and at the mouth. If someone is smiling with their whole face, you can usually guarantee they are sincere.

If a person is smiling straighter and has very tight lips, this could mean they are uncomfortable or not genuine.

Another indicator of an insincere smile is that they don't involve the eyes. The mouth and the eyes will be incongruent.

If a smile is joined by lasting direct eye contact, this can indicate that the person is attracted to you.

Eye blinking, pupil dilation, gaze direction, and eye blocking

Blinking too much or rapidly blinking shows nervousness or stress.

While we can't control our pupils, dilated pupils show interest or excitement.

Direct eye contact shows attentiveness and engagement, but too much direct eye contact can be seen as aggressive.

Eye blocking, which means covering or averting your eyes, is interpreted as discomfort or possible deception.

Positioning of the arms

Crossed arms can indicate defensiveness, resistance, or disagreement, while open and relaxed arms show openness, receptiveness, and confidence.

Other behaviors to look out for include putting an arm behind the back to create distance or holding something against the chest - these can all indicate discomfort and self-protection.

Positioning of the legs and feet

Like crossed arms, crossed legs can indicate defensiveness or a closed stance.

Believe it or not, even our feet can communicate! Feet pointing towards someone shows interest and engagement, but feet turned away (even if the body is not) can show disinterest or discomfort.

Positioning of the hands

Clenching your fists or tightening your hands shows tension, frustration, or aggression.

Open palms show honesty, openness, and non-threatening intentions.

Someone instinctively touching their own cheek may unconsciously communicate that they are thinking carefully or are very interested in what you are saying.

Distance

Close proximity to others can often indicate intimacy or a sense of comfort within another person's company. However, other social cues should be carefully considered because they can also indicate aggression.

Keeping a distance from others can indicate discomfort or disengagement.

Personal space boundaries vary significantly by culture and individual preference, so take cues from others and practice respect in every situation.

Taking Up Space

Sitting comfortably with legs and arms spread wide communicates that a person confidently dominates their space and gives others a perceived status of leadership and power.

The same can be accomplished using wide-sweeping gestures where smaller ones would be expected. Use this posturing wisely when you need to project competence and authority.

Culture

Many elements can alter the perception of body language. As with facial expressions, cultural differences should be carefully considered. A gesture, a form of eye contact, or a body position interpreted as positive or friendly in one culture can be seen as offensive or aggressive in another. If you interact with another culture frequently, it's a good idea to research that culture's nonverbal cues. If you are going to another country, research what types of body language are encouraged and what types to avoid to have the most positive experience possible.

Neurodiversity and Psychological Differences

Two other elements are developmental and psychological differences. Healthline (2020) notes, "Neurodiverse people may also use and interpret body language differently than neurotypical people do." For example, there are often nonverbal cues that someone wants to end a conversation - a neurodiverse person might miss those cues and continue the conversation past its natural end. People with psychological differences might experience similar issues. When having a conversation with someone who is neurodiverse or has psychological differences, have patience, practice empathy, and be aware of boundaries some people may have around nonverbal communication, like eye contact or casual touch.

> **Take Action:**
> **Posture Awareness Exercise**: Set an alarm for various times throughout the day. Each time it rings, check and correct your posture. Note any changes in your mood or how others perceive you.

Analyzing Tone

You may have heard the expression before, "It's not what you say; it's how you say it." How we say something has much to do with our tone of voice. Although tone is something you can hear, it is considered an element of nonverbal communication. Tone can communicate a speaker's emotions, intentions, and attitudes through the pace or speed of speech, pitch, and rhythm.

If you want to bring more depth to your communication or help understand the message of others, understanding tone can help you become a better communicator. Customers First Academy (2024) states, "When our tone isn't aligned with our words, it can create confusion and misinterpretation. This is why it's so important to be conscious of how we communicate and ensure that the tone aligns with our message." Humans communicate with each other in many different ways. How you say things are just as important as what you say. Your tone of voice can make a difference in getting your message across to others. Below is a list of elements of vocal tone that affect communication.

A Deep Voice: Conveys authority, confidence, and strength, often commanding attention and respect.

A Soft and Quiet Tone: Suggests intimacy, sincerity, and vulnerability, inviting listeners to lean in and pay closer attention.

A Firm and Confident Tone: Exudes conviction, decisiveness, and assurance, instilling confidence in the speaker's message and leadership.

Calm Breathing: Indicates composure, relaxation, and control, fostering a sense of stability and reassurance.

Short, Quick Breaths: May suggest nervousness, excitement, or agitation, reflecting a heightened state of arousal.

Deep, Strong Breathing: Reflects confidence, vitality, and vigor, signaling physical and emotional well-being.

Using a Normal Volume: Conveys neutrality and balance, ensuring the message is heard without overpowering or subduing.

A Loud Tone: Commands attention and authority but may also convey aggression or intensity if not appropriately moderated.

A Whispered Tone: Creates intimacy and confidentiality, often used for sharing secrets or private conversations.

Rapid Speech: Indicates excitement, urgency, or anxiety but may also lead to decreased clarity and comprehension.

Slow and Deliberate Speech: Suggests thoughtfulness, precision, and control, enhancing clarity and emphasis on critical points.

Irregular Speech Speed: This may signal confusion, distraction, or emotional volatility, hindering communication and understanding.

Well-defined Articulation: Enhances clarity and precision, ensuring that words are easily understood and interpreted.

Overly Emphasized Articulation: This may come across as artificial or insincere, diminishing the authenticity and credibility of the message.

Imprecise and Stumbling Speech: Indicates uncertainty, nervousness, or lack of confidence, detracting from the message's clarity and impact.

Tone is an aspect of nonverbal communication you may not usually notice. However, there are several things you can do to use tone effectively in communication. First, you should make sure that your message matches your tone. If you are giving a compliment, make sure your voice is upbeat. If you are making a complaint, ensuring your tone is empathetic but firm can help you get what you want out of the situation.

Another way to use tone effectively in communication is to ensure that you speak clearly and concisely. Customers First Academy (2024) says, "When we are clear and concise with our words, it makes it easier for the other person to understand what we're saying. And since the tone of voice conveys emotion, clarity can help prevent any misinterpretation of our tone." Finally, being friendly is a highly undervalued aspect of communication these days. Using a tone that the other person interprets as pleasant and likable can help us build trust more quickly and create a positive connection. If you can say something warmly or otherwise, choose to be warm. It wins many subconscious advantages with your dialogue partner.

Mastering Non-Verbal Communication Yourself

So far in this chapter, you have learned about nonverbal communication, decoding facial expressions, understanding body language, and analyzing tone of voice. Armed with your new knowledge, you can now put it to use to master nonverbal communication for yourself. If you feel like you haven't mastered it yet, don't worry; effective non-verbal communication is a skill you can practice and develop over time. By increasing your awareness and control of non-verbal cues, you can enhance your interpersonal interactions, build rapport, and convey messages with clarity and impact. Here are some detailed tips on how to improve nonverbal communication skills.

Look for incongruent behaviors

If you are talking to someone and their behaviors do not match their words, it can communicate the truth behind the words being spoken. This may not be a malicious act. For example, if you have a friend you know struggling but is saying everything is 'great!', pay attention to what they communicate through their body. What is their facial expression? Are they making good eye contact? Is their body position communicating discomfort? Pay attention to all of their nonverbal cues; if they are incongruent with their words, probe further.

Use signals to add meaning

Very Well Mind (2022) states, "Remember that verbal and nonverbal communication work together to convey a message. You can improve your spoken communication by using body language that reinforces and supports what you are saying." So, just as you watch for incongruent verbal and nonverbal messages, ensure your nonverbal matches the message you want to convey.

Consider context

When communicating, consider the context and what nonverbal behavior is typical or appropriate in that setting. What is suitable with your friends on a night out may not be appropriate at a work event or a more formal social setting.

Look at signals as a whole

The different aspects of communication all work together to create a whole. Looking at and focusing on a single element alone can lead you to an incorrect conclusion. For example, imagine that a person sounds and looks confident in their words and body language, but you notice that they don't make much eye contact. If you were to decide based on the lack of eye contact alone, you might conclude that they were anxious or unsure. However, it's possible they were tired, distracted, or had some physical problem with their eyes that made eye contact difficult.

Know that signals can easily be misread by yourself and others

Interpreting nonverbal communication is only sometimes straightforward and requires interpersonal skills and emotional intelligence. Because it is so complex, signals can be misread at times. When interpreting someone's nonverbal skills, look for a group of behaviors and overall behavior. If you feel that you have given off a signal that has been misread, work to correct it either through your words or nonverbal signals.

Know how to manage stress in the moment

If you feel stressed while communicating, managing your stress effectively can help you communicate better and improve your nonverbal. If speaking makes you nervous, especially in front of a group, take some long, deep breaths before communicating to help calm your body and mind.

Use hand gestures wisely

Some people speak with their hands more than others; I am guilty of this habit. However, overusing hand gestures can make you appear overstimulated or out of control. Pay attention to your hand gestures to ensure they are intentional and meaningful. Hand gestures should reinforce meaning and not create confusion.

Practice

Some people are natural communicators born with the gift of effectively and correctly communicating and interpreting communication from others. If you are not one of these people, you can work towards becoming a better communicator by practicing good communication behaviors. Pay careful attention to nonverbal behaviors and practice nonverbal communication with others.

One thing that can be helpful if you are improving your nonverbal communication skills is to practice Mirroring. Mirroring is when you observe the behavior of others and reflect the behavior to them. According to Science of People (2024), "Mirroring, also known as mimicking or Gauchais Reaction, is a nonverbal technique where a person copies the body language, vocal qualities, or attitude of another person.

Mirroring can occur throughout a social interaction and often goes unnoticed." Mirroring can be natural and unconscious; however, you can also practice it deliberately. Studies have shown that Mirroring can build trust and deepen relationships. It has even been show to increase the likelihood of positive outcomes in negotiations or sales situations.

To practice Mirroring, you must first pay careful attention to how the other person communicates. Mirroring should feel natural and subtle, so spend a reasonable amount of time observing so your attempt at

Mirroring doesn't read as insincere or incongruent. Don't attempt to precisely mimic the person you are speaking to because that can make the person you are speaking to feel like you are mimicking or making fun of them.

You can verbally mirror by moving towards matching tone, pace, pitch, volume, phrasing, or inflection in your speech. You can mirror body language by Mirroring non-verbal communication, including posture, stance, hand gestures, and facial expressions. Like any form of conversation, it can't be forced or faked, but a little awareness and practice can help us become more skilled at sparking connections with others.

In this chapter, we explored how to analyze the elements of non-verbal communication to help you read between the lines while listening to others speak. We also discussed how to communicate effectively nonverbally to help you show more confidence and make your message more compelling through your facial expressions, body language, gestures, and vocal tone.

This concludes Part II: Developing Practical Social and Communication Skills. We hope you have picked up some tools to help you talk to anyone! Part III will introduce you to some revolutionary communication tactics. The next chapter will use empathy and emotional intelligence to craft stronger connections. We'll also help you learn ways to develop and enhance your empathy and emotional intelligence.

***

Ending With a Bang!

Seize the moment and take decisive action to accelerate your progress. Swiftly implement the following steps to maximize your growth.

1. **Master the Power of Silence**: In your next few conversations, deliberately pause after the other person speaks. Observe how these moments of silence can deepen the conversation and improve your communication skills.

2. **Engage in People Watching**: Spend time in a public area, observing interactions without listening. Try to infer the context of conversations based on non-verbal cues alone. Record your observations and verify them if possible.

3. **Professional Non-Verbal Audit**: During a professional meeting, note your own and others' non-verbal cues. Reflect on how these might be influencing the meeting's dynamics.

4. **Teach Someone**: Explain the concept of non-verbal communication to someone unfamiliar with it, using real-life examples to illustrate each essential element.

May I Ask A Favor?

Hey there, Awesome Reader!

You've stumbled upon the middle of this book and haven't thrown it out the window. Congratulations! May I ask a tiny favor? Would you please pop over to the link below and write a review? Think of it as Yelp, but instead of reviewing a pizza place, you're helping the underappreciated world of words!

I know what you're thinking: "But I'm not a writer." Don't worry, neither am I! Just kidding, but seriously, it only takes a sentence or two. Something like, "This book is helpful because..." or "Five stars because this author gets me. I recommend."

Your review not only boosts my book's performance but also helps me prove to my relatives that I have a real job. Plus, every time you write a review, a writer gets their wings! (Not really, but one can dream, right?)

Who knows? Your words could be the reason someone picks up this book and finds the help they desperately need.

Thanks a million, and if you ever see me in public, pretend this never happened.

Keep reading!

Jack

Link to Review:
https://posg.life/ReviewTalkToAnyone

Part III: Revolutionary Communication Tactics
Chapters 7 – 9

"The two words 'information' and 'communication' are often used interchangeably, but they signify quite different things. Information is giving out; communication is getting through." — Sydney J. Harris

Chapter 7
Mastering the Art of Heartstrings and Handshakes

S ome people make communicating look easy. They take on any social interaction with a sense of confidence and excitement. They communicate effortlessly and make the person they talk to feel heard, ensuring they listen well. If you're not that person yet, don't worry; throughout this book, you've already learned some essential skills to help you get there! In this chapter, we'll explore a few more practices that go beyond the surface level of simply being able to speak and listen. We'll discuss some underlying skills and traits to help you talk to anyone.

Empathy and emotional intelligence are essential when communicating and forming or maintaining connections. Elena Aguilar (2018) wrote in her article "The Power of Empathy" how she discovered the power of empathy in her classroom. Aguilar had been struggling with a particular student she calls T.

T was constantly frustrated and defiant and challenged Aguilar daily. Aguilar said, "She refused to do anything and skirted the border of being disruptive. Week after week, I'd try to connect with her, but she put up a big wall around herself. In response, I felt myself closing up."

One day, a simple writing prompt broke open Aguilar's empathy for T. She asked her students to write about what one wish they would want to be granted if they had found a genie in a bottle. Her student, T, wrote candidly about the harsh reality of her life, which was marked by poverty and family conflict.

Her one wish was for clothes because she had recently bought most of what she owned, and her family couldn't afford to get her anything new. From that writing prompt, Aguilar began a dialogue with T that helped create a better relationship profoundly impacted by empathy.

Empathy and emotional intelligence are tools for understanding and sources of strength and resilience. Empathy can help you make that interaction successful for you and others when faced with a challenging social interaction. When you have empathy and emotional intelligence, you can see beyond the words exchanged in a conversation and get to the heart of the matter. These tools in the social skills toolbox will help you communicate with others in revolutionary ways and create a better social environment—one connection at a time.

Understanding Empathy and Emotional Intelligence

What is empathy?

Empathy and sympathy are often confused aspects of understanding and communication. While sympathy involves pity for others, empathy goes beyond a simple feeling and illustrates a sense of awareness of someone else's feelings.

We've all heard the phrase, "Put yourself in someone else's shoes." What the phrase truly reflects is the ability to understand things from the perspective of another. Empathy is sharing someone else's feelings and knowing why they are having them.

Whether or not you are experiencing sympathy or genuine empathy can be challenging to pinpoint. Empathy doesn't always come naturally, but there are signs you can look for to help you figure out if you are empathetic.

- Are you a good listener?

- Do people often feel comfortable coming to you with their problems or for advice?

- Do you usually think about the feelings of others?

- If you hear about a tragic event, do you feel overwhelmed?

- Can you quickly tell if someone is lying?

- Do social situations drain your battery?

You're probably empathetic if you answered yes to some or all of these questions! Below, we'll discuss the different types of empathy and some common barriers to experiencing or expressing it.

Different Types of Empathy

Cognitive empathy: Cognitive empathy refers to conscious mental activities. It is the ability to understand someone else's feelings logically. Very Well Mind (2024) states, "Cognitive empathy involves being able to understand another person's mental state and what they might be thinking in response to the situation."

Affective empathy: The word affective relates to a person's feelings or attitudes. Affective empathy reflects someone's ability to understand someone else's feelings emotionally. Berkeley University (2024) describes this: "Affective empathy refers to the sensations and feelings we get in response to others' emotions; this can include mirroring what that person is feeling, or just feeling stressed when we detect another's fear or anxiety."

Somatic empathy: Somatic refers to something physical that affects the body instead of the mind. Somatic empathy can involve a bodily experience of what someone else is feeling. For example, if someone close to you feels embarrassed, you might begin blushing or crying when you see someone else cry.

Barriers to Experiencing and Expressing Empathy

If everyone could always experience a healthy amount of empathy, the world might be a better place. However, barriers often prevent us from feeling empathy, even when we otherwise might. Knowing about these barriers can help us overcome them.

Cognitive biases: As discussed above, the word cognitive reflects our mental processes. A cognitive bias is deeply ingrained in our brains and has created a way of processing facts and information. This may have been a perspective that was taught to you in childhood, and it can be challenging to overcome. For example, you may have heard your parents or other trusted adults say that homelessness is due to laziness. If you have formed this cognitive bias in your brain, it may make it difficult for you to feel empathy for a homeless person because of your cognitive bias.

Dehumanization: Dehumanization refers to seeing others as inherently different from yourself to the extent that they begin to lose their human qualities. Very Well Mind (2024) states, "Many also fall victim to the trap of thinking that people who are different don't feel and behave the same as they do. This is particularly common in cases when other people are physically distant." So, for example, if you see a news report of something tragic that happened in a country or culture that is very different from yours, you may struggle to empathize with those people more than you would if it happened in your own country or culture.

Victim blaming: Another common barrier to empathy is victim blaming. An example is seeing a crime victim and wondering or asking them what they did to make the crime happen to them or what they might have done to prevent it. This is especially common if you know both the victim and perpetrator. As human beings, we are compelled to seek out justice. In other words, we have an innate sense that everyone should get what they deserve. So, if something terrible happens to someone, we might believe they did something to deserve it. This way, we can justify the event and feel safe that we won't fall victim to something similar.

Empathy is not a skill you are born with; it's developed over time, and there are barriers like those we discussed above that can prevent us from feeling empathy for others even if we want to. With the knowledge of the different types of empathy and the barriers you must overcome, you can begin practicing and honing your empathic skills.

Time to take some ground:
Reflect on Your Experiences: Write a journal entry about a time someone demonstrated deep empathy towards you and how it impacted your relationship. Reflect on how this experience made you feel and why it was significant.

What is Emotional Intelligence?

While IQ refers to someone's ability to process information cognitively, Emotional Intelligence, sometimes called EQ, refers to the ability to process and manage emotions. This can include both your own emotions and those of others. Psychology Today (2024) is defined as "The ability to recognize, interpret, and regulate your own emotions and understand those of others. Emotional intelligence skills allow for better personal well-being and interpersonal relationships." Cultivating your emotional intelligence can offer you a range of benefits, from making relationships easier to navigate to helping you gain more success in your career. Below, you will find a list of the various components of emotional intelligence.

The Components of Emotional Intelligence

Perceiving emotions: The first component includes the ability to accurately recognize and interpret emotions, including facial expressions, body language, and vocal cues.

Reasoning with emotions: Next is the capacity to use emotions to facilitate thinking and problem-solving. This will also include integrating emotional awareness into decision-making processes.

Understanding emotions: This is the skill of comprehending the complex nature of emotions, including their causes, triggers, and effects on behavior and relationships.

Managing emotions: When we effectively manage emotions, we can regulate and control our feelings in various situations and constructively influence the emotions of others.

Self-awareness: Self-awareness means a deep understanding of one's own emotions, strengths, weaknesses, values, and goals, leading to greater self-confidence and authenticity.

Self-regulation: The capability to effectively manage and control one's impulses, emotions, and reactions, even in challenging or stressful circumstances, is known as self-regulation.

Social skills: This involves proficiency in building and maintaining positive relationships, communicating effectively, resolving conflicts, and collaborating with others. Emotional intelligence and social skills go hand in hand to build one's capability to interact with and relate to others.

Empathy: You've got this one down by now! Empathy is the capacity to understand and share the feelings and perspectives of others, showing compassion and sensitivity to their emotions and experiences.

Motivation: The inner desire to set and pursue meaningful goals, persist in the face of obstacles, and strive for personal and professional growth is motivation.

Some signs of emotional intelligence include the ability to identify and name your own emotions and harness them in constructive ways. For example, you can apply your feelings to everyday problems to create a positive result or use your EQ skills to help regulate or manage others' emotional reactions successfully.

There are ways to measure your EQ. Tests like the Mayer-Salovey-Caruso Emotional Intelligence Test (MSCEIT) or the Emotional and Social Competence Inventory (ESCI) can help you better understand your level of emotional intelligence. These tests measure your EQ through self-reporting and are usually done professionally. The questions are behavior-based, and you respond to questions about how you would behave in different situations. There are also informal tests and quizzes that you can take online. While the results may be less accurate, they can give you a broad idea of whether or not your EQ is high or if you need to dedicate some time to work on it.

Like empathy, emotional intelligence is a skill that can be developed over time. There are vital skills that you can practice to help you both be more empathic and raise your emotional intelligence. In the following sections, we'll give tips and action steps for improving these critical social skills.

How to Develop Your Empathy

Developing empathy can be as simple as being willing to grow. You can increase your empathy by listening, asking questions, and being curious about another person. If you believe you are capable of empathy (we all are) and dedicate yourself to focusing on developing it, there are actions you can take to help you along the way. Below are five steps you can take right now and some additional tips to help you develop your empathy.

How to Develop Empathy

Step 1: Don't Assume You Understand

When conversing with someone struggling, don't assume you understand what they are going through, even if you have experienced something similar—instead, focus on your reflective listening practices. Summarize what you heard them say and note any emotions that you noticed.

For example, you might say, "It sounds like your mother is ill, and you are struggling with taking care of her while managing your other responsibilities. It sounds like you are both sad and frustrated; is that correct?" The speaker will then have a chance to clarify the situation or their feelings, and you'll get the opportunity to understand them better and empathize with the problem.

Step 2: Stay Present

Active listening can help you fully engage in the conversation and pay attention to verbal and non-verbal cues. Avoid distractions as much as possible. If the speaker says something you resonate with or that triggers a similar memory, resist the urge to blur the lines between your experience and theirs. Ask questions about their experience and practice, seeking their unique perspective.

Step 3: Manage your Filters

Humans naturally look for similarities in others and try to sync their beliefs with their experiences to help them understand the world around them. Understand your cognitive biases so you don't tune out what contradicts your views. Open yourself up to other ideas and opinions. Be on the lookout for new and enriching experiences. Don't rush to judgment - you never know when you might learn something new!

Step 4: Don't Commiserate

While it's natural to want to relate to someone else's experiences, resist the urge to turn the conversation back to yourself. Instead of sharing about similar experiences, focus on validating the other person's feelings and experiences. If you are conversing with others and they are making a judgment, don't jump to an agreement - ask questions to find out how they came to feel that way and why.

Step 5: Remember the goal is to understand their perspective, not fix their problem.

"You should . . . " is one way to stop a conversation in its tracks but shutting down the other person. It can also block you from feeling empathy for someone else because it can lead to victim-blaming and dehumanization. Empathy is about connecting with someone emotionally and understanding their perspective. Rather than jump in and give advice, take the time to listen, offer support, and validate their feelings before bombarding them with proposed solutions.

Additional Tips for Developing Empathy

Make listening a priority.

You can't connect with what another person is feeling without first figuring out what that feeling is. Practice active listening and strategic questioning to help you dive deeper into their emotions. Very Well Mind (2024) notes, "Empathy begins when you set the intention of listening for emotion. Make an effort to notice the signals people are giving that can indicate what they are feeling."

Share feelings.

By "sharing feelings," we don't necessarily mean to share our feelings with others (although this is a healthy practice!). Instead, we intend to take on some or a part of another person's emotions. Put aside what you would feel in that situation and try to pinpoint how it makes them feel. See if you can relate to how they are feeling and why. When you are willing to take on the part of someone else's pain, you can stand next to them and support them more empathetically.

Be vulnerable.

Allowing yourself to be vulnerable and empathetic towards others shows empathy by acknowledging your own struggles and demonstrating compassion towards theirs. Being vulnerable helps you understand why empathy is valuable to others and gives you essential support during tough times. If you empathize when they need it most, you should also be willing to accept it in return.

Take action and offer help.

Empathy does not end with sharing or listening to feelings. Empathy often requires action to truly support another person. If you listen with empathy, you can identify someone else's needs and actively work to help them. Very Well Mind (2024) describes it this way, "The key advantage of knowing what another person is going through is that you can better identify what other people need. Because empathy means that you are adopting the emotion but not the tough situation that gave rise to it, you are usually in a more empowered place to help."

Take Massive Action:
Empathy in Action: Volunteer at a local organization and keep a diary of your experiences. Focus on moments where empathy was required and describe how you responded.

How to Enhance Your Emotional Intelligence

Like empathy, you can also work to develop your emotional intelligence. Remember that learning how to improve your emotional intelligence is just the beginning. Help Guide (2024) states, "Just because you know you should do something doesn't mean you will—especially when you become overwhelmed by stress, which can override your best intentions. In order to permanently change behavior in ways that stand up under pressure, you need to learn how to overcome stress in the moment and in your relationships to remain emotionally aware." You can work on the following emotional intelligence elements to improve your EQ and social skills.

Element 1: Self-regulation

Self-regulation refers to the ability to regulate your emotional state. The following are ways that you can improve your self-regulation:

Identify your Triggers: Are there specific things that make you angry or lash out? Will you let a negative incident ruin your entire day? Everyone has their own triggers; how we react to them reflects our EQ level. However, you can learn to self-regulate when you face a trigger and keep your emotions in check.

Pause and Reflect: When faced with a trigger, take a beat and pause before you allow yourself to react. Initial reactions are often based on pure emotions and without logic. Taking a moment to pause and reflect can help calm you before responding impulsively.

Practice Mindfulness: Mindful techniques like deep breathing or meditation can help you better regulate your emotions and keep you present in the moment. If a conversation or situation is causing your emotions to run amok, feel empowered to give yourself a break so that you can regulate and return to the conversation later.

Developing Coping Strategies: You can experiment with coping strategies like journaling, mindful walking, or talking your emotions out with a professional or trusted friend. These strategies can help you manage stress and make self-regulation of your emotions more manageable.

Element 2: Self-Awareness

Self-awareness is the ability to recognize and understand one's emotions. It may involve what one feels in a particular moment or a longer-term overall emotion, like loneliness or depression. Below are some strategies to help one become more self-aware.

Reflect on Your Emotions: Give yourself the time and space to reflect on your thoughts and feelings. This can help you identify more prolonged emotions or feelings you may need help addressing. It can also help you to process painful situations. Reflect so you can correctly identify the emotion and attempt to pinpoint a cause.

Seek Feedback: If you want to know more about how others perceive your emotional responses, ask trusted friends, family, or colleagues for feedback on how they perceive your responses in emotional situations. They can give you valuable insight that will help you become more self-aware.

Practice Self-Assessment: Use journals, self-assessment quizzes, or other tools to explore your emotional strengths, weaknesses, values, and goals. These strategies help you process situations where you may have struggled and become more aware of how you might want to react.

Stay Curious: Approach self-awareness as an ongoing journey of self-discovery, remaining open to new insights and perspectives about yourself.

Element 3: Social Awareness

Turn self-awareness around, and you have social awareness. This means being able to recognize and understand others' emotions. Below, you'll find ways to improve your social awareness and grow your EQ.

Practice Active Listening: When interacting with others, practice active listening skills to help you better understand their perspectives and emotions. Active listening can help you recognize verbal and nonverbal cues that will help you recognize others' feelings.

Observe Social Dynamics: Sometimes, it's helpful to sit back and observe the dynamics of a group. It can help you to pick up cues in different situations and adapt your behavior accordingly. This can lead to more positive relationships and help you to integrate into new groups of people more easily.

Learn from Diverse Perspectives: Seek opportunities to interact with people from different backgrounds. This can broaden your perspective and increase your understanding of others, which can help improve your EQ and empathy.

Element 4: Relationship management

If you want to go beyond awareness and build your EQ to make you a better friend, family member, or colleague, then learning how to manage relationships can help you reach your goal. Here are some strategies to help you get there:

Communicate Effectively: Be intentional. Practicing clear and assertive communication can help you express yourself respectfully, an essential key to managing your relationships. Being open with others reduces misunderstandings and can help build a better and more meaningful relationship.

Resolve Conflicts Constructively: Many people fear conflict; however, it can be an opportunity for relationship growth and understanding. Effective conflict management not only helps you manage your relationships but can also make you a better leader and more successful in the workplace.

Build Trust: Building trust with others helps to build rapport. Demonstrating that you are consistently trustworthy will give you a reputation for integrity and reliability. Trust is a crucial element of any good relationship, and having trust will help make managing relationships easier.

Increasing your emotional intelligence is a process that takes time. However, by remaining open and curious, being willing to look inside yourself to identify your emotions, and allowing yourself to recognize a variety of perspectives, you can take steps towards improving this set of social skills. If you keep a growth mindset, you can learn from your experiences and raise your emotional intelligence in ways that will benefit your mental well-being and relationships with others.

How These Social Skills Nurture Stronger Connections

Empathy and emotional intelligence are crucial in fostering and maintaining healthy relationships across various contexts. According to Intelligent Change (2024), emotional intelligence can give us sensitivity that we might otherwise lack. They state, "The deep understanding of emotions, sensitivity to signals of emotional shifts, total engagement in a relationship, and, finally, emotional stability and life satisfaction are the main benefits of developing emotional intelligence skills." Empathy, of course, is a significant part of being emotionally intelligent and helps to create a safe space for others to be their authentic selves and form more meaningful relationships.

In a romantic relationship, this might take the form of a partnership where both people can better manage their conflicts, communicate more openly, and practice empathy with one another. Romantic relationships with emotionally intelligent and empathetic partners will be healthier overall and more fulfilling due to increased intimacy, trust, and respect.

In friendships, emotional intelligence and empathy can enhance the quality of the relationship through mutual understanding, the ability to successfully regulate emotions, and empathize with friends' feelings and experiences. People tend to avoid friendships with people who lack authenticity, and people who are willing to be open and authentic are entirely more enjoyable. Emotional intelligence and empathy will foster mutually supporting and long-lasting connections.

At work, emotional intelligence and empathy are critical factors for success. Workplace dynamics can be tricky, and workplace conflict can damage your career if you lack the skill to navigate it effectively. Emotional intelligence and empathy will help enhance your workplace communication skills and ability to work as a team. It also improves your leadership abilities, which can help you grow through the ranks and foster career success.

Finally, emotional intelligence and empathy are vital in new relationships. At the beginning of any relationship, you should seek to lay a foundation of emotionally healthy communication and boundaries. Practicing your emotional intelligence and empathy skills can help you do just that and enable you to begin a fully authentic relationship.

Cultivating your emotional intelligence and empathy skills can help you better understand and interact with others. These skills can give you deeper emotional connections and help you build more meaningful relationships. They help create the foundation of a healthy relationship. They are two more tools for your social skills toolbox that can enrich your relationships and help you talk to anyone!

In this chapter, we discussed the roles of empathy and emotional intelligence in communicating and forming or maintaining connections with others. We explored numerous ways you can help develop your empathy and emotional intelligence skills. These are excellent for building your social toolbox and helping you easily interact with others.

In the next chapter, we'll discuss how to set effective boundaries in a respectful way that protects others' feelings. Good boundaries are essential for both your mental well-being and your relationship health. You'll learn about them and how to develop your boundary-setting skills with empathy and self-care as the focus.

***

Ending With a Bang!

Seize the moment and take massive action to accelerate your personal progress. The key is to act swiftly and decisively on the following steps.

1. Emotion Tracking: Maintain an emotion diary for a week documenting each significant emotion felt and its context. Analyze the triggers and responses.

2. Emotion Regulation Practice: Next time you feel a strong emotion write down the steps you take to calm yourself before responding. Evaluate the effectiveness of these steps.

3. Somatic Empathy Tuning: When interacting with others note your physical reactions to their emotional expressions. Reflect on how your body's responses could inform your understanding of their feelings.

4. **Practice Assertive Communication**: Record a conversation where you focus on expressing your needs clearly without aggression. Reflect on the interaction and how the clarity of communication affected the outcome.

Chapter 8
Saying "No" With Diplomacy and Strength

In a book about how to talk to anyone, you may wonder how saying no and setting boundaries fits in! However, setting healthy boundaries and knowing when to say no is vital to good social skills and self-care. It creates a space where you can protect both your emotional and physical well-being. Without boundaries, you risk giving away all your emotional and social energy to others and missing out on opportunities to recharge your social battery.

In this chapter, we'll discuss the importance of boundaries and explain how to set effective boundaries without hurting the feelings of others. You'll gain a deeper understanding of the part boundaries play in helping you create healthier relationships while maintaining a solid sense of self.

Cassie had always been the go-to person in her circle for anyone needing a favor, advice, or a listening ear. She took pride in her reputation as a generous and always available friend, but it was also a source of profound exhaustion. She rarely said no, fearing it would tarnish the image others held of her. This constant need to please had left her drained, with little time or energy for her own needs.

The turning point came during a hectic week. Between her full-time job and volunteering commitments, Cassie's schedule was packed. It was then that her friend, Zoe, called, asking for help to organize a last-minute birthday party for another friend. Normally, Cassie would have jumped at the opportunity, pushing her own priorities aside. But this time, something inside her snapped. She realized that she was neglecting her own well-being by constantly putting others first.

Taking a deep breath, Cassie explained to Zoe that while she loved helping and being available for her friends, she needed to prioritize her commitments that week. She suggested alternatives, like participating in a group planning app, and offered to help with some tasks remotely. Initially, Cassie worried that Zoe would be upset or that it would damage their friendship. Instead, Zoe was understanding and appreciative of Cassie's honesty.

This experience was liberating for Cassie. It was the first time she had set a boundary to protect her time and energy, and the world didn't fall apart. Instead, she found a deeper respect for herself and noticed that her relationships didn't suffer; they actually grew more truthful and authentic. Cassie learned the importance of balancing generosity towards others with care for herself. Setting healthy boundaries became a critical part of her social skills, allowing her to maintain her generosity without sacrificing her own well-being.

The Importance of Boundaries

Do you have trouble saying no? Have you ever felt like other people invade your personal mental and physical space, drain your energy, or walk all over you? If so, you may need some help with setting boundaries. According to Psych Central (2024), "A boundary is a rule or limit you set with another person to express what you deem acceptable and unacceptable. When you build good boundaries with others, you state your needs and wants in an assertive but not aggressive way. You may also discuss things you don't like or feel comfortable with." Below is a list and explanation of some of the most common boundaries.

The Different Types of Boundaries

Emotional boundaries – This type protects your feelings. When you set an emotional boundary, you may be limiting the kind of information you want to share or the people you want to be vulnerable with. For example, you might not want to talk about your personal life or past at work. If someone asks you to probe questions, you might say, "I'm uncomfortable talking about that."

Material boundaries –This type of boundary reflects how you want people to interact with your belongings or spaces. For example, you might not be comfortable lending your things to others, or you might wish others to remove their shoes when they enter your home. It could also reflect boundaries regarding your finances. You can set a boundary on what others know about your financial situation or on saying no to others if they ask to borrow money.

Intellectual boundaries – How you feel about discussing your thoughts, beliefs, and ideas reflects your intellectual boundaries. Some people will talk about anything, but if you have areas of discomfort, it's okay to set a boundary. Some common topics people set boundaries on are politics or religion because these beliefs can be very personal and sometimes lead to heated discussions.

Physical boundaries – A physical boundary consists of how you want to allow others to interact with your body or your space. You should never feel uncomfortable about how someone else touches or comes close to you. Physical boundaries keep you physically and mentally safe.

Time boundaries – How you spend your time can be an area where it can sometimes feel that you lack control. Work, family obligations, and house or yard work constantly demand our attention. Setting healthy boundaries on how others use your time will affect how stressed or how fulfilled you feel by the end of the day. You may need better time

                    JACK WOLF

boundaries regarding work-life balance, family time, sleep, or self-care to protect your mental well-being.

Relationship boundaries – This type of boundary reflects how you connect with others. You might integrate other boundaries within your relationship boundaries – like emotional, physical, or time. This type of boundary will help you avoid toxic relationship patterns and help you to cultivate better relationships and deeper connections.

You are not the only one who will benefit from setting healthy boundaries; your relationships will also benefit – even if they can't see that initially. When you take the time to communicate your thoughts, feelings, and needs, you enable those around you to do the same. This will help to prevent resentment because everyone's needs are known. It creates the space and time needed for everyone in the relationship to care for themselves. It also helps everyone to hold on to their independence. Healthy boundaries in relationships can improve your overall mental well-being. It's an essential tool for emotional regulation and keeping you happy and secure with both yourself and your relationships.

Time to Take Action:
Reflect on Your Own Needs: Write down three areas in your life where more explicit boundaries could reduce stress. Detail how these boundaries would improve your well-being.

8 Reasons Why Boundaries are Important in Relationships

1. **You won't be as likely to be taken advantage of**
   Setting boundaries will empower you to maintain healthy relationships by limiting what you are willing to give to others in specific situations.

2. **You'll be less likely to feel relationship burnout**
   Boundaries help you to understand your own limits and needs

in relationships, which will help you protect your energy, avoid exhaustion, and fulfill your needs.

3. **You'll form more positive and fulfilling relationships**
In the long run, setting and respecting the boundaries of others will make everyone more comfortable because it eliminates the unknown. When there are clear expectations, you remove all the guesswork and help relationships to thrive.

4. **You can safeguard your space both emotionally and physically**
Setting healthy boundaries will protect your emotional and physical well-being by ensuring that you have the space and time you need for self-care.

5. **You'll maintain a separation between your thoughts, feelings, and needs from those you have relationships with**
Independence and individuality are a healthy part of any good relationship, and being your most authentic self will only enhance your connections with others.

6. **You will prevent conflict**
When you clearly communicate your boundaries, you will eliminate the need to discuss them, minimizing the likelihood of conflicts. Good boundaries leave nothing left to fight about.

7. **You will develop a better sense of self-identity, worth, and respect**
Setting healthy boundaries places a high value on your own needs, which will help you value yourself more.

8. **You will become more independent**
Good boundaries will help you grow! They will encourage you to take responsibility for your own happiness and mental well-being.

How to Effectively Set Boundaries Without Hurting Any Feelings

If setting boundaries is new to you, you might be worried about how they will affect others. Setting boundaries can be difficult, and it takes time for everyone to adjust once new boundaries are in place. To help you get started, review the steps below to help you set healthy boundaries while maintaining relationships.

Step 1: Reflect

Consider the reasons for your boundaries. Why is it important to you to set these new boundaries? Spend some time reflecting on your reasons and motivations so you can explain if asked. Also, keeping your reasons in mind will help you stick to your decision if others resist your boundaries.

Step 2: Start Early and Begin Small

Setting boundaries at the beginning of a relationship will help you build a stronger foundation and create a deeper connection. Starting with just a few boundaries will let you see how setting a boundary makes you feel. It also enables you to evaluate and make adjustments according to the results. You can work at your own pace and adjust as you go.

Step 3: Use Assertive Communication

When communicating a boundary, it's crucial to use clear, firm, and respectful communication. Express your boundaries so that the other person can understand you, but also in a way that clarifies that you will not waver in your position.

Step 4: Work on Maintaining your Boundaries.

It's easy to let a boundary slip over time, and maintaining boundaries can be especially difficult if you are dealing with someone who doesn't respect them. However, remaining consistent will help reinforce the boundary and let the other person know you won't give in to their pressure or manipulation. When maintaining a boundary becomes difficult, return to step one and reflect on your why.

Step 5: Communicate when a Boundary is Crossed.

If you have set clear boundaries in a relationship and someone crosses them, be sure to communicate to that person that they have done so. You don't necessarily need to be confrontational or approach that person with anger. Try to point out the behavior while re-communicating the boundary that they crossed.

Boundaries can be set in any relationship, not just friendships and romantic relationships. It's common to hear of workplace drama. Setting firm boundaries with coworkers can help your mental well-being and work-life balance. You can even set boundaries with casual acquaintances or strangers. Setting a boundary establishes the standard for how you are willing to be treated, which can be done anywhere or anytime. Below are a few more tips to help you set boundaries successfully.

- Carve out time for yourself. Giving yourself some alone time can help you reflect, rest, and reset. This will better prepare you for setting and maintaining appropriate boundaries.

- Spend time doing things you enjoy to increase your self-worth and fill your self-love tank. This will help you feel that you are worthy of the protection boundaries provide.

- Don't be afraid to include extra boundaries – even if some cultural or organizational boundaries are in place (like at work). Just because outside boundaries exist, your personal boundaries still have value and should be honored.

Respecting the boundaries of others is just as important as setting and upholding your own boundaries. It would be unfair to expect others to respect your boundaries as you walk all over theirs. Given this example, those whose boundaries you disrespect will be much less likely to respect yours. Healthy boundaries will allow each person within a relationship to communicate their thoughts, feelings, and needs. Unhealthy boundaries can turn into abuse. If you are in a relationship with unhealthy boundaries, you can begin by trying to set healthier ones. However, if the other person in the relationship doesn't accept this change, you may want to consider taking a break or ending the relationship altogether.

Change Your Future:

Feedback Collection: After setting a boundary, have a feedback session with the person involved to discuss how the communication process felt for both sides.

How to Balance Empathy and Assertiveness

It is essential to balance empathy and assertiveness when communicating with others. When communicating a boundary, use your active listening skills to gain the other person's perspectives and feelings. Accepting a boundary can be challenging for the other person, and they may just want their own thoughts and feelings to be heard. You can also use "I" statements to focus the communication on how you feel rather than their behavior. For example, instead of saying, "You never respect my time." You could say, "I feel exhausted and angry when my time is not respected."

Consider your body language when you are communicating a boundary. Confident and non-threatening body language will help you assertively communicate while maintaining empathy. Finally, put yourself in the other person's shoes to help you be more empathic. This boundary might take them by surprise, and they may feel negatively.

You don't have to support their behavior if they act out toward you. Remember that setting the boundary means you still want this person in your life but want certain behaviors to stop. If you set boundaries assertively and empathetically, you will ultimately construct a stronger relationship with a deeper connection, enhanced trust, and more respect.

For more focused attention on the topic of boundaries, or if you need to talk to someone regarding your next steps, please refer to the resources available at https://posg.life/boundaries.

***

Ending With a Bang!

Take massive action to gain the most impact on personal progress. Do the following as quickly as possible.

1. **Boundary Reinforcement:** Write down a plan for what steps to take when a boundary is ignored, including specific phrases to use and actions to reinforce the boundary.

2. **Practice Saying 'No':** Choose a day to consciously practice saying no to requests that conflict with your priorities and reflect on the emotional outcomes.

3. **Experiment with Comfort Levels:** Deliberately put yourself in a situation where you must say no and reflect on the experience to build confidence.

4. **Re-evaluate Relationships:** Assess your relationships and determine which ones respect your boundaries and which do not. Plan actions for those that need change.

Chapter 9
Cultivating Unwavering Trust

I t's easy to talk to someone if trust is a part of the conversation. Trust is crucial to any healthy relationship and will help you form more profound and meaningful connections. Trust allows us to rely on one another and to feel secure in our interactions while fostering a sense of comfort, openness, and honesty. When you trust someone, you will feel more willing to take risks, share your feelings and thoughts, and seek help when needed. In this chapter, we'll discuss the importance of trust in relationships and how to build trust organically - to help you talk to anyone!

Natalie Benson tells her story of how trust helped her relationship with her husband in a 2023 Reader's Digest article about the power of trust. Natalie had a difficult time during the last election cycle. She became obsessed with politics, constantly scrolling for and distracted by political news. It didn't end after the election, and her anxiety reached an all-time high. When this began causing conflict in her marriage, her husband decided it was time to talk. He asked her to sit down for a chat and, trying his best not to be accusatory, expressed concern for her behavior change. He was worried, felt she had lost control of herself, and suggested that she go to see a therapist.

Of course, none of that was easy to hear. But this wasn't random criticism from a stranger. It was words of concern from the person who knew and loved her most. She loved him, too, but more importantly, she trusted him. Their relationship was built on a solid foundation of trust, and she knew that though she was feeling defensive, he wanted the best for her.

Because of their trust, Natalie could put aside her defensiveness and seek help. Her interest in politics had turned into dangerously obsessive behavior that was making her both physically and mentally unwell. Through the help of her husband and a therapist, Natalie was able to disengage and re-engage with those around her and find relief from the anxiety and obsessive behaviors that she was struggling with, all because of the trusting relationship she had built with her husband.

The Science and Value of Trust

Trust, or the belief or confidence one has in another person's reliability, integrity, and honesty, is essential because it provides a sense of security and safety in a relationship, allowing individuals to feel comfortable and vulnerable with each other. Luke Chang, Ph.D., discusses the science behind and the value of trust in his paper, "The Science of Trust." He states, "First, cooperation can be rewarding. Second, betrayal of trust can result in negative psychological value and make it less likely to trust even if there is an expectation of reciprocation. Third, we can often infer a relationship partner's motivations and receive value from reciprocating a relationship partner's good intentions." Having trust enhances the overall quality of the relationship. When you trust another person - whether they are a partner, a friend, a coworker, or a family member - you believe that there is meaning and truth behind their words.

Trust also means forgiveness and accountability when it is broken. The Healthy (2023) states, "Humans are fallible and will make mistakes which inevitably break the trust between two people. The key to a strong relationship is how this tear in the relationship is repaired. An apology, changed behavior, and kind words are a good start to repairing any tear." Trust is essential at all relationship stages because of the safe space it provides, even if we fall. It can also promote the following:

Positivity: When you trust another person, you become more open, giving, and overlooking shortcomings. You will feel more positive about the other person, yourself, and the world around you because you know that someone out there has your back.

Reduced Conflict: Trust in another person creates an ally, and when you feel you are working with an ally rather than an enemy, you are more likely to seek solutions that can help reduce conflict. You will be much less likely to suspect or doubt each other, creating a better environment where disputes can be resolved more efficiently and effectively.

Increased Closeness: When you trust another person, you are more likely to share your thoughts, feelings, and experiences. This sharing helps build a deeper connection, bringing you closer emotionally and strengthening your bond. When trust is the foundation, the sense of safety you feel with that person will bring you closer together.

A lack of trust can have a devastating impact on relationships. Open communication and mutual respect will halt when you don't trust another person. This can lead to conflict and make an emotional connection difficult. A lack of trust can create insecurity, eroding a relationship's sense of safety and stability. A lack of trust can also have an impact on your mental health and lead to side effects like depression, anxiety, concentration issues, and loneliness. Ultimately, without trust, your relationships can become strained and distant, affecting your ability to sustain the relationship over the long term.

Trust is not automatic in a relationship; it builds over time. Distrust can form over time, too, through small actions like when a person makes promises or commitments. It can also take shape quickly if the break in trust is enormous. Chang notes, "In general, trust will quickly decay once there has been a breach in a relationship. Dissolution of trust decays proportional to the degree to which an expectation of trust was violated." In other words, the worse the action, the more likely you will distrust the person.

Practice Transparency: Honesty can be a challenge for those who fear conflict or struggle with people-pleasing. Make a commitment to be open and honest in your communications today, noting any changes in your interactions and how others respond.

If you want to prevent distrust from forming in your relationships, there are some steps you can take to help you along the way. First, be upfront about your feelings, thoughts, and intentions, and also be willing to listen to the other person's concerns. Also, demonstrate that you can be counted on! This means following through on your promises and commitments and being there for the person when they need you. And finally, respect the other person's boundaries. As we discussed in the last chapter, showing that you are attentive to another person's needs and respecting the boundaries they put in place will show how much you value them.

How to Build Trust Organically

While it's true that trust can take time to develop, there are many things you can do to build trust organically and establish a deeper, more meaningful connection with the people in your life. Below, you'll find some simple and effective strategies for building trust in your relationships naturally and authentically to create solid and lasting relationships that enrich your life.

Be honest and open.

Communicating honestly and openly can feel uncomfortable at times, but withholding information or being dishonest can result in a betrayal of trust. Being open and honest can reduce misunderstandings and conflict.

Gradually become vulnerable.

Being vulnerable with another person can be terrifying, but vulnerability is critical to building trust. Building trust often requires gradual steps towards vulnerability as you become more comfortable with each other. If you can let your guard down and be authentic, the other person may trust you enough to show their feelings, too.

Remember the role of respect.

Treating others with kindness, consideration, and respect will make you more likely to build trust. When building trust, the worst thing you can do is to belittle the other person's feelings or speak to them condescendingly. Acknowledging other's needs, perspectives, emotions, and boundaries will foster mutual respect between you.

Give the benefit of the doubt.

If you have already earned trust in the other person, assuming they have good intentions can further strengthen that trust. Making unfounded assumptions about someone's intentions or actions can increase distrust and damage relationships. Trust involves believing your partner has your best interests, even when misunderstandings or disagreements arise. Instead of making assumptions, seek clarification when needed and communicate openly.

Express feelings functionally.

As stated above, effective communication can help you build trust, including communicating your feelings constructively. Practicing active listening, using "I feel . . ." statements, and validating your partner's feelings can all help you to communicate in ways that will build trust.

Be willing to give as well as receive.

Reciprocity means exchanging for the sake of mutual benefit. When you have a relationship of any kind with an exchange of feelings and care, you build more trust and feel closer to that person. Trust is a two-way street. You can show that you are trustworthy by supporting their needs and aspirations and accepting their support.

Be willing to listen.

When you listen, you show that you understand. You can also show that you value and respect the other person. Not listening, of course, can produce the opposite effect. Practice active listening and show empathy by being attentive without interrupting or being dismissive.

Take time to make decisions.

When you take your time making decisions, you remove emotional factors that can lead to impulsive behavior. Also, thoughtfully considering the impact of your choices on a relationship demonstrates respect and consideration for the other person, which can lead to more trust and a better connection.

Don't take your relationship for granted.

If you want a relationship to grow through building trust, valuing and appreciating the relationship by investing time and effort will nurture it. When you put other things or people first, it sends the message that the person you are trying to build a better relationship with that they do not matter. Instead, you can demonstrate how much you value someone by focusing on them and making small gestures of appreciation.

Prioritize quality time.

These days, it seems we are all just getting busier and busier. However, spending meaningful time together can deepen your connection and strengthen trust in a relationship. Even if you only have a little time, engaging in activities you both enjoy and creating shared experiences will help reinforce your bond and build trust.

Have regular check-ins.

Regular check-ins provide an opportunity to express your feelings and needs. This could be a weekly date night if you are working on a romantic relationship. If you are trying to build trust with a family member, this could be done by scheduled phone calls. Either way, if you set aside some time to check in with the other person so that you can express yourself transparently and honestly, you can build trust by putting in a specific and planned effort to check in on the other person's feelings and progress.

Take accountability for your actions.

Accept responsibility for mistakes or shortcomings and apologize when necessary. When you take accountability, you show that you have the self-awareness to admit when you are wrong. Sharing these difficult moments with someone you are building trust with shows your maturity and ability to be trustworthy in good times and bad.

Follow through and be consistent.

Even the most minor actions can have a significant impact if done consistently. Consistently honoring your promises and commitments shows that you are reliable and predictable. You can build trust by demonstrating that you can be counted on to deliver on your word.

Be willing to forgive.

Forgiving doesn't necessarily translate to agreeing with the person's past behavior. You can practice forgiveness and let go of past grievances or resentments because holding onto grudges only hinders trust and prevents healing. By forgiving another person when they do something wrong, you can cultivate a mindset of compassion and understanding. This will give the relationship the space to grow and an increased sense of trust.

When discussing building trust, many first think of building trust with a romantic partner. However, trust is essential in every kind of relationship because of the healthy connections it creates. Trust is necessary for relationships to avoid insecurity, communication barriers, and conflict, hindering your potential for personal growth and fulfillment.

One relationship that should be considered when building trust is our relationship with ourselves. Self-trust involves prioritizing your personal feelings, needs, and sense of safety. It reflects the amount of trust you have in yourself to take care of yourself in everyday situations and challenging times. Practicing self-trust involves being self-aware and cultivating a deep sense of confidence in your abilities and judgment. Setting realistic goals, making and honoring commitments, being kind to yourself, and learning from your mistakes can all help you build your self-trust. Trusting in yourself can help you grow and feel more fulfilled, making your other relationships more meaningful.

Reflect on Past Trust: Write about an experience where trust was broken. Reflect on what happened, how it affected you, and what could have been done differently. Use this reflection to guide how you handle trust moving forward.

Building Trust in Professional Relationships

Building trust in professional relationships is as important as in personal relationships. Trust can help you create successful collaborations and a positive work environment. It reduces workplace drama and can prevent conflicts and misunderstandings. Trust can help you work together more effectively with your coworkers and clients, leading to increased productivity, job satisfaction, and stronger connections in your professional network.

Robert had recently joined the marketing team of a well-known corporation, bringing with him a wealth of industry experience but finding himself amidst colleagues who were closely knit and somewhat wary of new members. Determined to build trust and integrate himself into the team, Robert embarked on a strategic approach that embodied the essence of effective workplace relationships.

From day one, Robert was meticulous about the promises he made. He knew his capacity and was clear about his commitments, ensuring he never overpromised or underdelivered. When an unforeseen challenge arose that threatened to delay a project deadline, he communicated this early to his team, explaining the situation and the steps he was taking to address it. This transparency helped minimize disappointments and build reliability.

Robert also made a concerted effort to communicate authentically. He avoided corporate jargon, choosing instead to speak and write in a way that was genuine and easy to understand. His interactions weren't just about work; he showed genuine interest in his colleagues' lives outside of the office, which opened the door to deeper, more meaningful conversations and a better understanding of each other's strengths and personalities.

He made it his mission to see the brilliance in every team member, often shining a spotlight on their contributions. It was a simple gesture, but it wove a strong fabric of appreciation and respect among the team. When he made a mistake, he was quick to admit it, demonstrating humility and a willingness to learn—qualities that greatly endeared him to his colleagues.

Robert's participation in office activities, whether in a brainstorming session or a casual team lunch, showed his dedication to the job and the people he worked with. His readiness to lend a hand, professionally or through personal support, solidified his colleagues' trust in him.

Finally, operating with unwavering values, Robert was the same person in the office as he was outside, his integrity and honesty shining through in every interaction. He steered clear of office politics and gossip, treating everyone with respect and kindness, thereby fostering an inclusive environment.

Robert's journey wasn't just about integrating into a team; it was about enriching the tapestry of workplace relationships with threads of trust, authenticity, and mutual respect. His story reminds us of the beauty of genuine connections in creating a workspace not just of colleagues but of friends and trusted confidants.

Keep Moving Forward:
Ask for Feedback: Request feedback on how you handle trust in relationships. Reflect on the feedback and plan how you can improve based on it.

Methods for Boosting Trust Within Professional Collaboration

Keep your promises—and if you can't communicate that early so that you don't overpromise or underdeliver.

Communicate frequently, functionally, and professionally - including written, verbal, and nonverbal communication. Avoid the temptation to be fake or practice corporate speaking. Be authentic while communicating clearly and concisely.

Show genuine interest in your team's lives. You will work better together and learn each other's strengths outside the workplace.

Be a mentor to someone. Sharing your prior knowledge about a company or an industry can benefit a newcomer while exposing you to new relationships and ideas.

See the value in each team member. Everyone has something to offer, and when you see the value in all team members, you acknowledge their work and worth.

Admit your mistakes. If you make a mistake at work, don't try to hide it. Admitting your mistakes will speak volumes about your character and allow you to learn from them.

Participate in office activities. Whether it's a brain-storming session, a team-building activity, or answering a question during mandatory training, participating in work-related activities will show that you care for both the company and the people in it.

Help your team. Build trust by helping others on your team when they need it. They will know they can count on you during challenging times, and the added trust will encourage them to reciprocate.

Operate with values. Your values inside the workplace should reflect your values outside of the workplace. Refrain from sacrificing your values to get ahead or appease leadership. Showing your coworkers that you have integrity and practice honestly will help build trust and create better workplace relationships.

Be inclusive. The workplace is often like high school, with its various cliques and groups. Avoid gossiping and be nice to everyone. Showing your maturity by being inclusive of others can help you build trust with everyone.

No matter the relationship, trust and the ability to build it have a profound significance in our lives. It binds relationships together and adds depth to our connections. Trust can help you navigate life's obstacles confidently because you know someone is out there to help you and provide a safe space for you if you need it.

***

Ending With a Bang!

Take massive action to gain the most impact on personal progress. Do the following as quickly as possible.

1. **Forgive Past Mistakes:** Actively forgive someone and reflect on how this forgiveness affects your feelings towards them and the overall relationship.

2. **Share Responsibilities:** Share a responsibility with a coworker or family member and reflect on how this shared experience affects your trust levels.

3. **Practice Transparency:** Commit to one day of complete honesty in all your interactions. Note any changes in how people respond and how it makes you feel.

4. **Give the Benefit of the Doubt:** During a disagreement, consciously decide to trust the other person's intentions—Journal about the situation and any changes in the conflict resolution.

Chapter 10
Transforming Your Work Connections into Career Gold

Marianne received a last-minute call to attend a leadership conference as a fill-in for a colleague who could no longer attend. Upon arrival, she headed to a table at the back of the room to take her seat. As she did this, another woman coming toward her joked that she was also trying to "hide at the back of the room." After introducing herself, Marianne realized she was speaking with a woman she had long admired and felt incredibly fortunate. The two women spent the event "hiding" at the back of the room together. They exchanged stories and insights, and Marianne learned so much from her admired colleague. Despite her success, she was amazed at how down-to-earth and approachable the woman was. That day, Marianne realized that sometimes the best opportunities come unexpectedly, and she left the conference feeling inspired and grateful for the chance encounter that allowed her to connect with such an admirable leader.

Being able to talk to others in your professional network is an essential social skill that can affect your future career advancement and success. You might be looking for new opportunities or valuable industry insight. You might want help with a challenge or need inspiration to help you grow in a new way. Whatever you are looking for, professional networking can help you build authentic and supportive relationships that can positively change your career. This chapter will discuss the value of networking and explain how to make an effective professional network for yourself. At the end of this chapter, you'll better understand how to harness this social skill to advance your career and achieve professional goals.

The Art and Science of Networking

Networking is when you build relationships and connections with others in a professional setting. When you network, you will meet and communicate with people to share ideas, information, and resources, expand your personal and professional opportunities, and grow as a grower. It doesn't always have to be a formal interaction, either. Networking can take place in small and unlikely ways, like during a break at a meeting or even in an elevator.

Networking lets you learn about new job openings, industry trends, and business developments. Investopedia (2023) says, "It helps a professional keep up with current events in the field and develops relationships that may boost future business or employment prospects." Also, the relationship between your professional connections and your ability to find a job in your desired industry is profound. Better Up (2023) reports, "Thirty-one percent of job seekers find listings through professional connections, especially referrals. Networking can open doors to new opportunities that might be out of reach otherwise." Whether you are seeking a new career or hoping to grow in your current one, establishing professional relationships through networking can give you allies that will help open doors for you.

There are ample opportunities to participate in networking activities in and out of the workplace. You could attend conferences or other industry events, join a professional organization, or connect with other people through social media platforms like LinkedIn. Good networking skills also involve effective communication skills, such as active listening, expressing ideas clearly, and building rapport with others. Learning how to network well can help you talk to anyone! Below are some more benefits that networking has to offer.

It improves social well-being.

Networking creates opportunities to form meaningful personal and professional connections. These connections help you feel a sense of belonging and community with your professional peers, leading to more happiness and fulfillment overall at your place of work.

It leads to the exchange of ideas.

When you bring together people who work in the same field or industry, you can encourage creativity and innovation by sharing ideas and feedback. You'll be able to find other people who have diverse perspectives and experiences who can be there to collaborate with you or inspire you.

It helps you meet people at various professional levels.

Networking is a great way to meet others who are at different career levels. You may meet a talented entry-level coworker you can help mentor or a seasoned executive who can help mentor you and get you to the next level. Networking is a great way to get and give guidance to and from others in your field.

It boosts your confidence.

Networking can boost your confidence by allowing you to showcase your skills and expertise to others. Your peers can help validate you and recognize your achievements. You can create a valuable support network that believes in you and your abilities.

It expands your visibility.

Networking can expand your visibility by increasing your professional reputation. Don't underestimate the power of an excellent professional reputation! You want your name to be known to others in your industry or field for all the good you have done or have the ability to do. This can help you open the door to future collaborations or career advancements you might not have had access to.

It helps you find inspiration.

Networking can expose you to others' success stories, motivating you to set ambitious goals. It can also encourage you to pursue your passions and focus on your vision.

It enhances career interests.

Connecting with other professionals with similar career aspirations can provide you with insights, resources, and opportunities. However, connecting with people in different fields and industries can help you make connections that will help you think outside the box and gain diverse perspectives. It could lead you down a path you hadn't thought of before.

You'll gain advice and support.

Networking with other professionals can be invaluable for advice and support. They can provide the guidance and constructive feedback you need to take your career to the next level and navigate the challenges you will face while trying to achieve your career goals.

It helps you develop long-term professional relationships.

Networking can help you develop long-term relationships. Trust and mutual respect can lead to decades-long collaborations or opportunities when these relationships are characterized by trust and mutual respect.

Take Action:
Joining a Professional Organization: Research and list three professional organizations relevant to your field. Note the benefits of joining each and decide on one to join this month.

How to Build a Powerful Professional Network

When building a professional network, you should undergo the process with intention and a strategic mindset. Because the professional relationships you build through networking can be such an essential factor in your career development, it's crucial to identify the people and relationships that will be most beneficial. According to The Balance (2019), "Many people don't know how to go about it, but networking isn't quite as complicated as it sounds. Even if you are just starting, you are already part of a network. The next step is to learn how to expand, maintain, and use it effectively."

How you build your network is primarily up to you. However, you should pay careful attention to the reputation of those with whom you are forming connections. Someone else's reputation or action can harm yours. Also, keep in mind that each new contact will lead to more, and if the foundation of your network is broken, it will put the building at risk of collapse. Your networking relationships should also be authentic. Find shared goals and interests and engage in meaningful conversations beyond small talk. Listen actively to show interest in what the other person has to say. Be genuine, respectful, and professional. Building authentic relationships with high-quality individuals will grow your professional network into a thriving support system.

Sam's Success Story

Sam was always the shy one—more comfortable behind a screen than in a crowded room. His journey from being a reserved individual to a networking pro is a testament to the power of stepping out of one's comfort zone and strategically leveraging professional networking.

Sam's first step was dedicating specific times in his schedule for networking. Every Wednesday evening, he would attend a webinar or a virtual meetup, ensuring he was consistent in his efforts to meet new people. Understanding the importance of giving as much as receiving,

Sam made it his mission to offer help to his peers. Whether it was sharing an insightful article or providing feedback on a project, Sam was there, building trust and forming genuine connections.

He quickly realized the significance of focusing on quality over quantity. Instead of trying to connect with everyone, Sam identified vital individuals who shared his goals and values. This approach led him to deeper, more meaningful relationships that were both professionally rewarding and personally fulfilling.

Sam placed a particular emphasis on one-to-one relationships. He invested time in personalized interactions, sending tailored messages to individuals he met online or at virtual events. These customized efforts paid off, as Sam found himself building a network of people who were not just contacts but potential friends and mentors.

Patience and persistence were Sam's mantras. He knew professional networking was a journey, not a sprint. He set clear goals for his networking efforts—whether it was learning about new industry trends or finding a mentor. This clarity helped him purposefully navigate events and interactions, making the most of his time and connections.

Recognizing his value was perhaps the most significant hurdle Sam had to overcome. Shy and reserved, he initially struggled to see what he could bring to the table. However, by acknowledging his unique skills and experiences, Sam gained the confidence to put himself out there. He created a list of individuals he wanted to reach out to and strategically selected contacts who aligned with his objectives.

Finally, Sam understood the importance of asking for help. He reached out to his network for advice, introductions, and assistance when needed, always with a genuine desire to reciprocate. His journey from a shy individual to a networking pro was not just about building a professional network; it was about growth, confidence, and the power of human connection.

Tips to Get Started

You can consider any or all of the following relationships when building your professional network - colleagues, members of professional associations, former instructors or professors, or even friends you already have within the same field. No matter who you are adding to your professional network, you may need more tips to help you work on how. Below, you'll find some additional tips to help you get started:

Dedicate time to professional networking. Setting aside a specific time in your schedule for networking will help you nurture new relationships. Be consistent in your actions to build and maintain your network over time.

Help your peers. As much as you can expect professional networking to benefit you, you should also be willing to offer support and assistance to others whenever you can. Being generous with your knowledge and resources can build trust with others in your professional community.

Focus on quality over quantity. While connecting with as many people as possible is a good idea, cultivating deep and meaningful relationships with a select group of individuals who align with your goals and values will produce better results.

Utilize social media. Don't overlook social media's ability to help you expand your network. Professionals use social media daily to share their insights and engage with other like-minded people. Actively participating in social media groups for your field can increase your visibility and credibility.

Join a college alum group. Your college or university is an excellent resource for connecting with fellow graduates with common goals and professional interests. Your college or university probably also has an alum group that hosts networking events to encourage you to form professional relationships through your alma mater.

Focus on one-to-one relationships. Invest time and effort in building individual connections through personalized interactions rather than relying solely on mass networking events or group settings. Customized relationships are more likely to be genuine and impactful.

Remember that professional networking is a journey. It is not a one-time action or event. It should be approached as a continuous process that requires patience and persistence because meaningful relationships, professional or otherwise, take time to nurture.

Know your goals. What are your networking objectives? You can develop your industry knowledge, find a mentor, or search for new career opportunities. Knowing your objectives will help you go into networking events with clear goals and prioritize your activities.

Acknowledge your value. Your unique skills, experiences, and perspectives are valuable, and you have much to offer other professionals! Confidence in your abilities will attract professional connections and help you find mutually beneficial professional relationships.

Create an outreach list. One problem with attending professional events or conferences is that often, you will meet more people than you can reasonably follow up with. Compile a list of individuals you want to connect with or reach out to for networking purposes. Be strategic in selecting contacts and focus on those who can help you achieve your goals.

Consider who you already know. The people who can help you the most may already be known to you. You can begin networking by reviewing your existing contacts, such as former colleagues, classmates, and friends. They can make excellent additions to your network and introduce you to new opportunities and connections within their networks.

Just say hi. Hopefully, this book has given you the knowledge and skills to put yourself out there and talk to new people. Be brave. Begin to initiate conversations, whether in person or online. A simple greeting can lead to meaningful discussions. Challenging yourself to step out of your comfort zone and talk to new people can create potential opportunities for collaboration or support.

Create and use memorable business cards. Business cards are a great way to help others remember you after you walk away. Design professional and memorable cards that accurately represent you and the professional image you want others to remember. Distributing them can facilitate follow-up communication.

Don't be afraid to ask others for help. When needed, contact your network for assistance, advice, or introductions. Most professionals are happy to help others, especially if you've built a genuine relationship with them.

Make It Happen:
Crafting Introductions: Practice writing an email asking a current contact to introduce you to someone else in their network. Include why you want to connect with that person and how it could be mutually beneficial.

Nurturing Your Network

Once you have grown a solid professional network, you must maintain it in an ongoing effort to keep it thriving. Here are a few tips to help you keep your network going.

Stay connected. Keep in touch with your professional network in whatever way possible - through email, phone, social media, or in person. Consistent communication with your network can strengthen your professional relationships and keep your network strong.

Help people in your network. Networking is about both giving and receiving. Supporting others in your network can help you practice your skills, brush up on your expertise, and often learn something completely new. Being generous and helpful reinforces reciprocity within your network and deepens your connections.

Revisit older connections. Periodically revisit older connections in your network, even if you haven't been in touch for some time. Catching up with your former connections can help you explore new opportunities for collaboration and support.

In conclusion, the art of networking is a critical skill for anyone looking to advance their career and widen their professional horizons. Throughout this chapter, we've explored how effective networking goes beyond mere social interactions—it's about building enduring, mutually beneficial relationships that can propel both your personal and professional development. By engaging authentically with others, fostering meaningful connections, and continuously nurturing these relationships, you lay the groundwork for a robust network supporting you through various career stages. Remember, the key to transforming your work connections into career gold lies in your ability to listen, learn, and contribute genuinely to the success of others. As you expand your network, keep these principles in mind, and watch as new doors of opportunity open, guiding you towards more extraordinary achievements and fulfillment in your career path.

✳✳✳

Ending With a Bang!

Seize the moment and take massive action to accelerate your personal progress. The key is to act swiftly and decisively on the following steps.

1. **Plan for a Networking Event**: Choose an upcoming networking event to attend. List three objectives you want to achieve from this event, like meeting specific people or gaining knowledge in a particular area.

2. **Goal-Setting for Networking**: Write specific networking goals for the next three months. Include the types of professionals you want to meet and what you hope to achieve from these connections.

3. **LinkedIn Profile Challenge**: Update or create your LinkedIn profile. Add a new professional photo, update your bio, and ensure your work experience is current. Share your profile link with a peer for feedback.

4. **Informational Interview Planner**: Identify two professionals you admire and draft an email requesting an informational interview. Include why you chose them and what you wish to learn from them.

Take the Plunge
Conclusion

Communicating and thriving in social situations can be intimidating for just about anyone. Even people who don't struggle with social anxiety can seek to improve their social and communication skills. But you don't have to struggle alone! The tips and strategies you learned in this book can help you begin a journey toward improvement.

If you want to succeed, you have to take action. You have all of the steps you need. Remember, there are additional resources and downloadable content on my website, https://posg.life, and advanced lessons on my podcast Life Sculptor Blueprint. You can contact me with any questions, and you can reach out to my Facebook page when you want feedback. You have the knowledge, tools, and support to get you through writing and launching your first book. You're not alone in this journey.

This book has been a journey of self-discovery for you, teaching you about your authentic self and boosting your confidence and self-esteem. You've made significant strides in learning how to start and maintain conversations, using active listening as a social tool, and reading and practicing effective nonverbal communication. In the final section, you also learned the importance of empathy, emotional intelligence, and boundaries. You've learned to trust in creating meaningful relationships and how to use networking to advance your career. Reflect on how far you've come and the skills you've developed. You're well on your way to mastering social and communication skills!

We began this book with the story of Dave, a 32-year-old Illinois man struggling to form relationships due to social anxiety. Dave committed to working on himself to help overcome his fear and create a better life with more meaningful relationships. With the tips, strategies, and activities in this book, you can overcome struggles with social and communication skills as Dave did. Now that you have all the confidence and social skills that you need to thrive in any social situation, all there is left for you to do is get out there and start engaging in enthralling conversations! Imagine the sense of accomplishment and fulfillment you'll feel when you do.

Don't Miss Your Last Chance

I'm a firm believer in second chances. Now that you've finished reading this book, I'm excited to offer you a series of bonuses. Visit the link below and enter your email address, and I'll instantly send you a link to my **Super-Secret Resources Page**. It's effortless and will amaze you.

You'll receive a few more emails with all the additional content I promised throughout the book. This includes some unique advanced training, custom content to further your journey in Talking To Anyone, Opportunities for quitting your job and becoming an entrepreneur, and even more insider strategies for transformational success.

Break out with extreme momentum. Supercharge your results today to accelerate your growth. You can turn down the volume of social anxiety and experience the thrill of increasing control over your life and talking to anyone.

https://posg.life/GetSecretAccess

More Information

I've mentioned several book titles, images, links, and extra resources throughout this book. You can conveniently access all of this content at the following:

https://posg.life/bestself

There is no need to recall any other links or names from the book. Just relax, enjoy the journey, and concentrate on shaping your future.

Join the Podcast

https://JackWolfPOSG.podbean.com

Join the **Life Sculptor Blueprint** podcast, your ultimate guide to shaping a thriving life and career. Hosted by Jack Wolf, this podcast delves into the art and science of personal transformation, offering you the tools to master social skills, boost emotional intelligence, enhance communication, sharpen critical thinking, cultivate success habits, and crush your business goals. Each episode is a treasure trove of actionable insights, expert interviews, and practical tips drawn from Jack's acclaimed book series, including How To Talk To Anyone, Critical Thinking for Know-It-Alls, Emotional Intelligence for Men, and Transformational Success Habits.

Whether you're looking to make a dazzling impression at your next social event or build your business with confidence, Jack's engaging style and wealth of knowledge will guide you every step of the way. Join us as we explore the secrets to unlocking your potential, fostering meaningful connections, and achieving unparalleled success in your personal and professional life. With **Life Sculptor Blueprint**, you're not just listening—you're crafting a better, bolder, and brighter future. Let's sculpt your life into a masterpiece!

About the Author
Jack Wolf

Jack Wolf, the self-proclaimed superhero of the self-help world—minus the cape and the tight spandex (thank goodness)—is a lighthouse for many in the stormy seas of life. His relatable journey and passion for words, which could rival a man-crush, turn every page he publishes into joy and hope for the soul.

As a reader, you would love to cozy up with Jack's warm writing on a cold night. You will appreciate his insight as your unofficial life coach. He dives deep into the human experience, surfacing with treasures of love, resilience, and the sheer fearlessness of the human spirit. His books? They're not just stories; they're life-altering lessons designed to 'Jack' up your spirits and transform your life.

As the head honcho at POSG, Inc., Jack's spreading his good-vibes-only policy like its literary confetti. This publishing group is like the cool kids' table where everyone's invited. From children's coloring books and stories to self-development or even religion, Jack wants to make the world a tad brighter with his words.

Jack's commitment to his craft and readers has him cultivating a fanbase so dedicated that they'd probably walk over LEGOs barefoot for his latest release. He's more than just a writer or a publisher; he's a mentor, entertainer, teacher, storyteller, and friend. Each book Jack writes and publishes is a heart-to-heart chat, an invitation to join him in a world where you don't just read books—you live them. So, buckle up because a ride with Jack Wolf will either be one wild, inspirational adventure, or it will cure your insomnia. Either way, you win!

Books by Jack Wolf

1. **How to Talk to Anyone - Social Skills Made Easy**
   Proven Strategies for Mastering Small Talk, Confident Speaking, Approachable Communication, and Networking Success

2. **How to Talk to Anyone - Social Skills Made Easy Workbook**
   A Companion to the Book by the Same Name

3. **Transformational Success Habits**
   A 30-Day Plan to Take Charge of Your Struggles in Personal Growth, Leadership Skills, and Finances

4. **Critical Thinking for Know-It-Alls**
   A Five-Step Guide to Smarter Decisions and Creative Breakthroughs, Even if You Think You Know Everything

5. **Emotional Intelligence for Men**
   Proven Steps to Self-Awareness, Emotional Literacy, and Leveraging Emotions for Effective Decision-Making and Team Dynamics

6. **Facing Dragons:**
   Fantasy Fable Meets Self-Improvement Guide for Mastering Personal Growth to Achieve Entrepreneurial Triumphs

7. **Lovable Cute Animals Coloring Book for Kids**
   50 captivating coloring pages, each brimming with lovable cartoon critters waiting to be brought to life by your child's colorful genius

8. **Fantasy Heroes and Dragons Coloring Book for Kids**
   50 Unique Images of friendly dragons, fierce heroes, and mischievous goblins. Perfect for young fans of fantasy and mythical tales

9. **What is the Bible?**
   Understand Its History, Find Personal Meaning, and Connect With Its Author

Discover a Typo?

D espite our best efforts to make this book perfect, occasional errors may occur. If you notice any mistakes, please inform me by visiting:

https://posg.life.com/typo

Your feedback is greatly appreciated and helps ensure that future readers have a seamless experience. Thank you for helping improve this book as you come alongside the grammar police and rid the world of pesky mistakes.

One Last Thing

Big thanks for powering through this book! Seriously, your support means the world—like, you're pretty much a superhero now. You've got the power to boost this book into the stratosphere of the digital world just by leaving a review. Yup, it's almost like your opinion has superpowers!

Picture this: The book is fresh in your brain, you're cozied up with your e-reader, and POW! A wild review opportunity appears on this page. If you could take a whopping minute (less time than it takes to microwave a marshmallow) to write a review, you'd be changing the course of history itself.

Did you know that new reviews are like the spinach to Popeye? They keep this book flexing strong on digital shelves. Whether it's a five-star slam dunk or a thoughtful critique, your words have the mojo to help others find the help they need and potentially love this book, too.

Just hit that star rating or scribble a few words. It's a small click for you, a giant leap for book-kind!

Thanks a ton for being awesome, and remember, every time you leave a review, this author does a happy dance. No pressure, though!

https://posg.life/reviewtalktoanyone

Keep being legendary,

Jack

References

White, J. (2023, February 7). 700 Inspiring Quotes About Building A Strong Foundation. Clarity. https://www.consultclarity.org/post/quotes-about-building-a-foundation

The Path to Unconditional Self-Acceptance. (n.d.). Psychology Today. https://www.psychologytoday.com/intl/blog/evolution-the-self/200809/the-path-unconditional-self-acceptance

Pillay, S. (2016, May 16). Greater self-acceptance improves emotional well-being - Harvard Health Blog. Harvard Health Blog. https://www.health.harvard.edu/blog/greater-self-acceptance-improves-emotional-well-201605169546

Gupta, S. (2022, September 14). What Is Self-Acceptance? Verywell Mind. https://www.verywellmind.com/self-acceptance-characteristics-importance-and-tips-for-improvement-6544468

Ackerman, C. (2018, July 12). What is Self-Acceptance? 25 Exercises + Definition and Quotes. PositivePsychology.com. https://positivepsychology.com/self-acceptance/

Waters, S. (2021, August 5). The path to self-acceptance. BetterUp. https://www.betterup.com/blog/self-acceptance

How to Practice Acceptance | Psychology Today. (n.d.). Www.psychologytoday.com. https://www.psychologytoday.com/us/blog/click-here-happiness/202108/how-practice-acceptance

Authenticity | Psychology Today United
     Kingdom. (n.d.). Www.psychologytoday.com.
     https://www.psychologytoday.com/gb/basics/authenticity
Dare to Be Yourself | Psychology Today United Kingdom. (n.d.).
     Www.psychologytoday.com. Retrieved January 25, 2024, from
     https://www.psychologytoday.com/gb/articles/200805/dare-be-you
     rself
Emily. (2023, August 18). Embracing Authenticity: Unleashing Personal
     Growth and Connection. Aaron Hall.
     https://aaronhall.com/insights/embracing-authenticity-unleashing-p
     ersonal-growth-and-connection/
Embracing Uniqueness: How To Discover and Celebrate Your Identity
     as a Unique Person - Transitions and Beginnings. (2023, June 12).
     Transitionsandbeginnings.com.
     https://transitionsandbeginnings.com/embracing-uniqueness-how-t
     o-discover-and-celebrate-your-identity-as-a-unique-person/
How to Be Yourself: 10 Essential Steps Toward Authenticity - Brilliantio.
     (2023, December 15). https://brilliantio.com/how-to-be-yourself/
Develop Authenticity: 20 Ways to Be a More Authentic Person |
     Psychology Today United Kingdom. (n.d.).
     Www.psychologytoday.com.
     https://www.psychologytoday.com/gb/blog/click-here-happiness/20
     1904/develop-authenticity-20-ways-be-more-authentic-person
Jhangiani, R., & Tarry, H. (2014, September 26). The Social Self: The
     Role of the Social Situation – Principles of Social Psychology – 1st
     International Edition. Opentextbc.ca.
     https://opentextbc.ca/socialpsychology/chapter/the-social-self-the-
     role-of-the-social-situation/

4.3 The Social Self: The Role of the Social Situation. (2015, October 27). Open.lib.umn.edu; University of Minnesota Libraries Publishing edition, 2015. This edition adapted from a work originally produced in 2010 by a publisher who has requested that it not receive attribution. https://open.lib.umn.edu/socialpsychology/chapter/4-3-the-social-self-the-role-of-the-social-situation/

Nickerson, C. (2021, September 22). Individualistic Cultures and Behavior - Simply Psychology. Www.simplypsychology.org. https://www.simplypsychology.org/what-are-individualistic-cultures.html

Henricks, T. (2019). Our Individuality: It's a Collective Thing. Psychology Today. https://www.psychologytoday.com/us/blog/the-pathways-experience/201910/our-individuality-its-collective-thing

12 tips for Overcoming shyness (and embracing Self-Acceptance). (2021, June 11). Healthline. https://www.healthline.com/health/mental-health/how-to-stop-being-shy

Clinic, C. (2023, November 27). Need help overcoming social anxiety? 6 tips from an expert. Cleveland Clinic. https://health.clevelandclinic.org/how-to-overcome-social-anxiety

Cuncic, A., MA. (2023, September 26). How to socialize when you have social anxiety disorder. Verywell Mind. https://www.verywellmind.com/talk-people-social-anxiety-disorder-3024390

Lovering, N. (2022, October 28). 21 Socialization Tips for People with Social Anxiety. Psych Central. https://psychcentral.com/anxiety/socialization-tips-for-people-with-social-anxiety

Mulvey, K. (2023, March 29). If your social anxiety flares up at work, keep these tips in your back pocket. Real Simple. https://www.realsimple.com/health/mind-mood/social-anxiety-at-work

Professional, C. C. M. (n.d.). Social anxiety disorder (Social phobia). Cleveland Clinic. https://my.clevelandclinic.org/health/diseases/22709-social-anxiety

Pugle, M. (2023, November 29). What is social anxiety? Verywell Health. https://www.verywellhealth.com/social-anxiety-5091930

Ready to overcome social anxiety? These 9 tips can help. (2021, May 26). Healthline. https://www.healthline.com/health/anxiety/how-to-get-over-social-anxiety

Social anxiety disorder: more than just shyness. (n.d.). National Institute of Mental Health (NIMH). https://www.nimh.nih.gov/health/publications/social-anxiety-disorder-more-than-just-shyness

5 simple steps to build your confidence. (2023, July 28). Psychology Today. Retrieved February 12, 2024, from https://www.psychologytoday.com/us/blog/the-path-to-passionate-happiness/202307/5-simple-steps-to-build-your-confidence

6 tips for Overcoming Self Doubt. (2022, January 29). Psychology Today. Retrieved February 12, 2024, from https://www.psychologytoday.com/us/blog/the-truth-about-exercise-addiction/202201/6-tips-overcoming-self-doubt

Abrams LCSW-R, A. (2017, March 27). *8 steps to improving your self-esteem*. Psychology Today. Retrieved February 12, 2024, from https://www.psychologytoday.com/us/blog/nurturing-self-compassion/201703/8-steps-improving-your-self-esteem

Being assertive: Reduce stress, communicate better. (2024, January 20). Mayo Clinic. https://www.mayoclinic.org/healthy-lifestyle/stress-management/in-depth/assertive/art-20044644

Clinic, C. (2023, December 14). *Constantly down on yourself? How to Stop Negative Self-Talk*. Cleveland Clinic. https://health.clevelandclinic.org/what-is-negative-self-talk-and-how-to-change-it

Cuncic, A., MA. (2024, January 16). *12 Ways to have More Confident Body language*. Verywell Mind. https://www.verywellmind.com/ten-ways-to-have-more-confident-body-language-3024855

How can I improve my self-esteem? (n.d.). Mind. https://www.mind.org.uk/information-support/types-of-mental-health-problems/self-esteem/tips-to-improve-your-self-esteem/

How I cured myself of Imposter Syndrome. (2022, April 7). Psychology Today. Retrieved February 12, 2024, from https://www.psychologytoday.com/us/blog/buoyant-life/202204/how-i-cured-myself-imposter-syndrome

How to transcend self-doubt and negative self-talk. (2023, March 20). Psychology Today. Retrieved February 12, 2024, from https://www.psychologytoday.com/us/blog/the-stories-we-tell/202303/how-to-transcend-self-doubt-and-negative-self-talk

Kristenson, S. (2022, November 1). *How to Stop Negative Self-Talk: A 14-Step Guide*. Happier Human. https://www.happierhuman.com/stop-negative-self-talk/

Lcsw, A. M. (2024, January 26). *How to be More confident: 9 tips that work*. Verywell Mind. https://www.verywellmind.com/how-to-boost-your-self-confidence-4163098

Montijo, S. (2021, December 14). *How to use positive affirmations for a fulfilling life*. Psych Central. https://psychcentral.com/health/what-are-positive-affirmations

Morin, A. (2023, May 30). *6 Proven ways to build confidence*. Psychology Today. Retrieved February 12, 2024, from https://www.psychologytoday.com/us/blog/what-mentally-strong-people-dont-do/202305/6-proven-ways-to-build-confidence

Positive affirmations: 30 affirmation examples to use daily. (n.d.). https://www.betterup.com/blog/positive-affirmations

Positive thinking: Stop negative self-talk to reduce stress. (2023, November 21). Mayo Clinic. https://www.mayoclinic.org/healthy-lifestyle/stress-management/in-depth/positive-thinking/art-20043950

Scott, E., PhD. (2023, September 26). *How to use assertive communication*. Verywell Mind. https://www.verywellmind.com/learn-assertive-communication-in-five-simple-steps-3144969

Self-esteem: Take steps to feel better about yourself. (2022, July 6). Mayo Clinic. https://www.mayoclinic.org/healthy-lifestyle/adult-health/in-depth/self-esteem/art-20045374

Selig, M. (2018, August 6). *11 ways to project confidence and be taken seriously*. Psychology Today. Retrieved February 12, 2024, from https://www.psychologytoday.com/us/blog/changepower/201808/11-ways-project-confidence-and-be-taken-seriously

Speakers Institute. (2020, March 10). *15 ways to fake it till you make it (How to project confidence even if you don't feel it)*. https://www.speakersinstitute.com/15-ways-to-fake-it-till-you-make-it-how-to-project-confidence-even-if-you-dont-feel-it/

Staff, C. (2023, November 29). *Assertive Communication: definition, examples, and tips*. Coursera. https://www.coursera.org/articles/assertive-communication

Wisner, W. (2023, January 26). *25 positive daily affirmations to recite for your mental health*. Verywell Mind. https://www.verywellmind.com/positive-daily-affirmations-7097067

Sander, V. (2022, May 4). 158 Communication Quotes (Categorized by Type). SocialSelf blog. https://socialself.com/blog/communication-quotes/#effective

"7 Secrets for Having Great Conversations." *Psychology Today*, 6 Oct. 2021, www.psychologytoday.com/us/blog/can-t-we-all-just-get-along/202110/7-secrets-having-great-conversations. Accessed 16 Feb. 2024.

Barbieri, Annalisa. "'Be Interested, Be Curious, Hear What's Not Said': How I Learned to Really Listen to People." *The Guardian*, 24 July 2021, www.theguardian.com/lifeandstyle/2021/jul/24/interested-curious-how-i-learned-to-really-listen-to-people

Birt, Jamie. "How to Keep a Conversations Going: Benefits and 10 Tips." *Indeed*, 30 Sept. 2022, www.indeed.com/career-advice/career-development/how-to-keep-a-conversation-going. Accessed 16 Feb. 2024.

Foulkes, Lucy. "How to Have More Meaningful Conversations." *Psyche*, 19 Jan. 2024, psyche.co/guides/how-to-have-more-meaningful-conversations

Granneman, Jenn. "4 Hacks for Introverts to Transform Small Talk Into Meaningful Conversation." *IntrovertDear.com*, 23 June 2023, introvertdear.com/news/introverts-5-hacks-to-turn-small-talk-into-meaningful-conversation

Gupta, Sanjana. "50 Deep Conversation Starters for Meaningful Connections." *Verywell Mind*, 28 June 2023, www.verywellmind.com/deep-conversation-starters-7548671

How to Connect With People: 10 Surefire Ways. www.betterup.com/blog/how-to-connect-with-people

Kerr, Natalie, Ph. D. "5 Ways to Make Deeper, More Authentic Connections." *Psychology Today*, 3 Sept. 2021, www.psychologytoday.com/us/blog/social-influence/202109/5-ways-make-deeper-more-authentic-connections. Accessed 16 Feb. 2024

Lebow, Hilary I. "45+ Deep Conversation Starters to Bond With Friends and Family." *Psych Central*, 16 Mar. 2022, psychcentral.com/health/deep-conversation-starters

Linda Ugelow. "Meaningful Conversation Starters as a Tool for Speaking Practice." *Linda Ugelow*, 17 Dec. 2023, www.lindaugelow.com/meaningful-conversation-starters

Morin, David A. "How to Keep a Conversation Going (With Examples) | SocialSelf." *SocialSelf*, 7 Apr. 2023, socialself.com/blog/the-5-best-ways-to-keep-a-conversation-going

Robson, David. "The Conversational Habits That Build Better Connections." *BBC Worklife*, 25 Feb. 2022, www.bbc.com/worklife/article/20211109-what-we-get-wrong-about-conversations

Simonis, Daisy. "5 Ways for Introverts to Turn Small Talk Into 'Deep' Talk." *IntrovertDear.com*, 19 Feb. 2021, introvertdear.com/news/5-ways-to-turn-small-talk-into-deep-talk

Webb, Janice, Ph. D. "How to Enjoy Small Talk and Deepen Your Conversations." *Psychology Today*, 30 Aug. 2022, www.psychologytoday.com/us/blog/childhood-emotional-neglect/202208/how-enjoy-small-talk-and-deepen-your-conversations. Accessed 16 Feb. 2024.

Ccs, Hailey Shafir M. Ed, Lcmhcs, Lcas,. "How to Be a Better Listener (Examples & Bad Habits to Break) | SocialSelf." *SocialSelf*, 5 Aug. 2022, socialself.com/blog/better-listener

Clinic, Cleveland. "7 Ways to Improve Your Active Listening Skills." *Cleveland Clinic*, 18 Dec. 2023, health.clevelandclinic.org/active-listening

Cuncic, Arlin, MA. "7 Active Listening Techniques for Better Communication." *Verywell Mind*, 12 Feb. 2024, www.verywellmind.com/what-is-active-listening-3024343

Katz, Neil, and Kevin McNulty. "Reflective Listening." *Maxwell School of Citizenship & Public Affairs*, 1994. *Syracuse University*, www.maxwell.syr.edu/docs/default-source/ektron-files/reflective-listening-neil-katz-and-kevin-mcnulty.pdf?sfvrsn=f1fa6672_7

Lebow, Hilary I. "Become a Better Listener: Active Listening." *Psych Central*, 28 Sept. 2021, psychcentral.com/lib/become-a-better-listener-active-listening

Lynch, Matthew. "What Is Reflective Listening? - the Edvocate." *The Edvocate*, 26 Mar. 2021, www.theedadvocate.org/what-is-reflective-listening

Morin, David A. "How to Keep a Conversation Going (With Examples) | SocialSelf." *SocialSelf*, 7 Apr. 2023, socialself.com/blog/the-5-best-ways-to-keep-a-conversation-going

O'Bryan, Amanda, PhD. "How to Practice Active Listening: 16 Examples & Techniques." *PositivePsychology.com*, 18 Jan. 2024, positivepsychology.com/active-listening-techniques

Staff, Coursera. "What Is Active Listening and How Can You Improve This Key Skill?" *Coursera*, 1 Dec. 2023, www.coursera.org/articles/active-listening

"100+ Wisdom-Filled Communication Quotes For Clearer Conversations" *The Quotes Archive, 30* Sep. 2023, https://thequotesarchive.com/communication-quotes/

Assertyve, T., & Assertyve, T. (2023, December 24). *Assertiveness and empathy: striking a balance.* ASSERTYVE. https://assertyve.org/assertiveness-and-empathy-striking-a-balance/

Bell, E., & Bell, E. (2022, April 1). Setting boundaries: Cassie's Story. *Brook.* https://www.brook.org.uk/your-life/setting-boundaries-cassies-story/

BetterHelp Editorial Team. (2024, February 29). *The Importance of Setting Boundaries: 10 benefits for you and your relationships | BetterHelp.* https://www.betterhelp.com/advice/general/the-importance-of-setting-boundaries-10-benefits-for-you-and-your-relationships/

Boundaries: What are they and how to create them | Wellness Center | University of Illinois Chicago. (n.d.). https://wellnesscenter.uic.edu/news-stories/boundaries-what-are-they-and-how-to-create-them/

Lmft, M. C. B. (2023, September 14). *How to set healthy boundaries with anyone.* Verywell Health. https://www.verywellhealth.com/setting-boundaries-5208802

Moore, M. (2022, September 8). *The importance of personal boundaries.* Psych Central. https://psychcentral.com/relationships/the-importance-of-personal-boundaries

Nash, J., PhD. (2024, February 27). *How to set healthy boundaries & Build positive relationships*. PositivePsychology.com. https://positivepsychology.com/great-self-care-setting-healthy-boundaries/

"7 Ways to Build Trust in a Relationship." *Psychology Today*, 12 Dec. 2018, www.psychologytoday.com/us/blog/friendship-20/201812/7-ways-build-trust-in-relationship. Accessed 16 Mar. 2024.

Birt, Jamie. "14 Tips for Building Trust at Work (and Why It Matters)." *Indeed*, 3 Feb. 2023, www.indeed.com/career-advice/career-development/building-trust. Accessed 16 Mar. 2024.

BPsySc, Heather Craig. "10 Ways to Build Trust in a Relationship." *PositivePsychology.com*, 27 Feb. 2024, positivepsychology.com/build-trust

Choosing Therapy. "How to Build Trust in a Relationship: 22 Tips." *Choosing Therapy*, 3 Dec. 2023, www.choosingtherapy.com/build-trust-relationship

Gupta, Sanjana. "Why Trust Matters in Your Relationship and How to Build It." *Verywell Mind*, 6 Dec. 2023, www.verywellmind.com/how-to-build-trust-in-a-relationship-5207611

Hilton Anderson, Charlotte. "These Extraordinary True Stories Will Remind You About the Power of Trust." *Reader's Digest*, 20 Jan. 2023, www.rd.com/list/true-stories-trust. Accessed 16 Mar. 2024.

Jolie Courtney, Nadine. "Trust in a Relationship: Why It's Important—and How to Build It." *The Healthy*, 21 July 2023, www.thehealthy.com/family/relationships/trust-in-a-relationship. Accessed 16 Mar. 2024.

Knight Commission on Trust, Media, and American Democracy, et al. *The Science of Trust*. July 2017, www.aspeninstitute.org/wp-content/uploads/2017/07/Chang.The-Science-of-Trust.pdf

Bertagnoli, Lisa. "Professional Networking: Why It Matters and How to Build Your Network." *Built In*, 19 Dec. 2022, builtin.com/career-development/professional-networking

Imlanz. "8 Stories That Prove Successful Networking Doesn'T Have to Be Boring | Institute of Managers and Leaders." *Institute of Managers and Leaders*, 26 Aug. 2016, managersandleaders.com.au/8-stories-that-prove-successful-ne tworking-doesnt-have-to-be-boring

Indeed Editorial Team. "10 Tips to Help You Network Like a Pro." *Indeed*, 16 Feb. 2023, www.indeed.com/career-advice/finding-a-job/network-like-a-p ro. Accessed 19 Mar. 2024.

---. "The Benefits of Networking: 14 Reasons To Start Your Network." *Indeed*, 20 July 2022, www.indeed.com/career-advice/career-development/benefit-of -networking. Accessed 19 Mar. 2024.

Kagan, Julia. "Networking: What It Is and How to Do It Successfully." *Investopedia*, 21 June 2022, www.investopedia.com/terms/n/networking.asp

McKay, Dawn Rosenberg. "How to Build and Maintain a Professional Network." *The Balance*, 30 May 2019, www.thebalancemoney.com/building-growing-and-maintaining- a-professional-network-525834

Moser, Leslie. "How to Build a Helpful and Well-Connected Professional Network From Scratch." *The Muse*, 21 July 2015, www.themuse.com/advice/how-to-build-a-helpful-and-wellcon nected-professional-network-from-scratch

Perry, E. (2023, May 15). What is networking and why is it so important? | BetterUp. Www.betterup.com. https://www.betterup.com/blog/networking

Staff, Coursera. "9 Networking Tips to Expand and Strengthen Your Network." *Coursera*, 5 Jan. 2024, www.coursera.org/articles/networking-tips

Team, The Michael Page. "Top 12 Benefits of Networking: Why Networking Is Important." *Michael Page*, 13 Feb. 2024, www.michaelpage.com.au/advice/career-advice/career-progression/top-12-benefits-networking-why-networking-important

What Is Networking, and Why Do You Need to Do It? | Columbia CCE. www.careereducation.columbia.edu/resources/what-networking-and-why-do-you-need-do-it

9 798224 630899